LAUDERDALE SUB:
MEMORIES OF A MEMPHIS NEIGHBORHOOD

Dr. Logan H. Westbrooks

2025

Cover photos: Dr. Logan H. Westbrooks, Bishop G. E. Patterson, James Neely Interstate BBQ (Photo: Rein T. Fertel 2008 from SouthernFoodways.org), Westbrooks family: Pearl, Alphonso, Shirley, Logan, & Gloria (Westbrooks family archives), Dr. Reginald Porter Sr. (Hawkins/Porter archives), and Donald Bryant (Photo: blog.musoscribe.com).

Accessible Cover Description: Six photos (five of them in color, one in gray scale) are arranged in a collage: five photos show one African American man mentioned above each, smiling, and one photo shows the Westbrooks family, all African American and smiling.

Cover Concept by Dr. Logan H. Westbrooks

Cover Design by LaRita Shelby

Additional Graphic Design by Jessica Godbee

ISBN: 978-0-9987822-5-6

LCCN Library of Congress Control Number 2025917074

Ascent Publishing

1902 5th Avenue

Los Angeles, CA 90018

©2025

DEDICATION

This book is dedicated to the families that resided in the Lauderdale Sub from the 1940s and to those who remain as recently as 2023. This neighborhood holds a rich history all its own.

It was a thriving and vibrant neighborhood with children playing and interacting with each other. Mindful adults were always on the ready to spot and correct misbehavior. It was lively, friendly, and very closely knit. Everybody knew each other and all were on speaking terms.

There was also the sweet and pleasant aroma of baking cookies coming from Dortch's Cookie Factory on Lauderdale Street, among so many other memories.

My friend Ronald Anderson put it best when he wrote these words:

We are a generation that will never come back.

A generation that walked to school and then walked back, in rain, wind, and snow. A generation that did their homework alone to get out as soon as possible to play in the street. A generation that spent all of their free time in the streets with their friends, who became friends for life. A generation that played hide-and seek when dark. A generation that could see the night sky and see constellations in the milky way after dark such as the big dipper, the little dipper, and the north star.

A generation that made mud cakes and collected sports cards. A generation that found, collected, washed, and returned empty

Coke bottles to the local grocery store for five cents each and then bought a Mountain Dew, Coca Cola, Pepsi, Baby Ruth or a box of Cracker Jacks with the money.

A generation who made paper toys with their hands and built skate trucks from broken skates before they built skateboards.

A generation who bought vinyl albums to play on record players, 45 RPM and 78 RPM before they built LP albums. A generation whose TV went off at midnight after playing the national anthem.

A generation that is passing and unfortunately will never return no matter how hard we try.

Excerpt from "We Are a Generation That Will Never Come Back" by Ronald Anderson.

QUOTES FROM LAUDERDALE SUB RESIDENTS AND DESCENDANTS

I'm glad that Logan has been able to pull together this book and for documenting our history of Black excellence. It's good for our family legacy and lineage. We need to get those stories out there and to have it told, because a lot of people don't know all the contributions that our parents and our grandparents have made.

—Cheryl "Cherie" Hall

Cheryl Hall is the granddaughter of Bishop W. A. Patterson Sr., daughter of Bishop Samuel Smith, great-niece of Bishop J. O. Patterson Sr., niece of Bishop G. E. Patterson, and cousin of Bishop J. O. Patterson Jr.

Our teachers at Lincoln, Booker T. Washington High School, and LeMoyne-Owen College told us what brought on segregation, Jim Crow, and economic discrimination. We needed to progress intellectually, economically, politically, physically, spiritually, and organizationally to defeat it, and we're still doing that. It's not over yet.

—Dr. James Bishop

I learned the value of community and being a participant in the community, because my family was very much involved in the community and trying to make the community a better place.

—Dr. Reginald Porter Sr.

You didn't set limits. You had to have high expectations. That's what happened in the neighborhood.

—Fredericka Hodges

Our family values centered on faith in God, honesty, education, and a good work ethic.

—Carrie Moore Black

There was not a whole lot of conversation about what we couldn't do. There was more conversation about what we were expected to do. The examples we had are to focus on your mission. What are your goals? What is it you have to do? Keep your focus on the goals that you want to accomplish, rather than focusing on the impediments that are in your way.

—Phoebe Weaver Williams, Esq.

In my opinion, I thought I had a wonderful childhood growing up in the neighborhood.

—Pearl Westbrooks Hines

There were Colored and White drinking fountains and Colored and White entrances marked on the buildings in some of the places in Lauderdale Sub and all around Memphis. Despite all of that, within our neighborhood everybody just cared for each other. Everybody knew each other and looked out for each other.

—Shirley Westbrooks Smith

We made sure that we carried ourselves in a manner that was not just respected in man's eyes but was respected in God's eyes.

—Reginald Smith

Hopefully because of this book, historians will find a rich story of faith, hard work, survival, and a stream of success that is a direct result of who lived in Lauderdale Sub, how they raised their families, and how they took the best of what they had and made it even better.

—Dr. Logan H. Westbrooks

MESSAGE FROM THE EDITOR

When Mr. Westbrooks first brought this project to my attention it was January 2023. He stated that he wanted to do a book on Lauderdale Sub. To which I replied: "What is that?" I had never heard the term in my life.

He informed me that was the name of his former neighborhood in Memphis, Tennessee. It's not to be confused with Lauderdale Court, where the famous Elvis Presley lived in another part of the city before he rose to fame. Lauderdale Sub is the same neighborhood of cozy houses that my grandparents moved to during the depression era after they relocated from Athens, Georgia. It's the neighborhood of the homestead of the Hawkins, Davenport, Porter, and Smith families. The families with whom I share DNA. The former home of my maternal grandparents, aunts, uncles, cousins, neighbors, and lifelong friends.

What is remarkable is that I knew the neighborhood by no other designation. It is where my family tree planted their roots of faith, love, education, and excellence. The legacies are still bearing fruit.

Mr. Westbrooks gave me a list of families that had resided there from the 1940s to the 1960s. He wanted to interview these individuals about their life in Lauderdale Sub. I was impressed by his pristine memory of names, streets, and events that shaped his life.

As a specialist in business, entertainment, education, and the arts, I have become a master strategist in executing content from concept to creation. I figured we could gather the interviews in six months, then begin transcriptions and expect publication by the end of the year 2023. Well, it ended up taking two years to coordinate schedules, research additional family connections, transcribe, format, and ultimately bring the book to manifestation.

I also did not expect what I would end up learning about my own family. I knew what they meant to me, but I had no idea how they impacted members of their community. I heard stories that were never told before about my grandmother and my aunts.

Upon learning what Mary Ann Borders Mitchell shared about my grandmother's version of a trip around the world, somehow it all made sense that her grandchildren would eventually live, work, and travel all around the world. Although she didn't have the means to regularly venture outside the state of Tennessee but by faith, she did. She was not the only one who laid the foundations of generational aspirations and excellence.

While I revered the opportunity to work with Mr. Westbrooks, I was in awe of the dynamic legacy of education, advocacy, and entrepreneurship in his family. I had long held the notion that whoever was going around and telling Black people that they were "less than" and what they "could not do" had somehow missed our street.

After spending two years working on this book and speaking to multiple generations from this same community that fostered my family values, I am now profoundly aware. There was a consensus. They were all steeped in faith, they lived by it, they raised their children by it, and they dared to reach for all that was possible for them despite any perils that were around them.

I have been blessed to receive many accolades in my life. Whenever I am complimented, I am quick to say: "If you only knew the people who raised me, you would know that I am nothing special. I am a mere reflection of what was lived before me, unceremoniously and unapologetically."

My family never informed me that their neighborhood had a name. I grew up traveling the streets that led to grandma's house: South Parkway, Person, Essex, McMillan, and Carnegie, where grandma lived. Oh, and where I'm from, Carnegie is pronounced with a soft g and sounds like j versus the pronunciation of Carnegie Hall.

This book is not an academic periodical. However, it is now a historical document that exemplifies the treasures that we hold in our oral traditions. Some of the families documented here can't be found anywhere else.

My sincere thanks to everyone who participated. I must note that my beloved first cousin Dank (also known as Rev. Dr. Reginald Lawrence Porter Sr.) passed away on December 24, 2024, much to our surprise. Thankfully, we were able to enshrine many of his fond childhood memories right here in this book.

As the saying goes, welcome to the neighborhood. Except for the few well-kept houses that remain, you'd never know from looking at it now exactly what it was then and the greatness that came out of it.

LaRita Shelby

Lauderdale Sub descendant, Editor, Creative Director, and Consultant for *Lauderdale Sub* by Dr. Logan H. Westbrooks

SPECIAL THANKS

This is a list of those who greatly added their time, talent, and memories to this book. First, I'd like to thank my beautiful wife Geri Douthet Westbrooks. Thank you to my nephew Reginald Smith, Alpha Westbrooks Allen, and my editor, creative consultant, project manager and Lauderdale Sub descendant LaRita Shelby.

Also, thanks to my team Delia Koen, Dr. Justin Key, Dee Robinson and author, educator, and Memphis historian Shirley Neely. Delia and Shirley are also Lauderdale Sub descendants. Thank you to structural editor and proofreader Ana Mourant and book formatter Wendy Mach. Also, thanks to Alison Ollivierre of Tombolo Maps and Design.

A special thanks goes to my sister Shirley for her pristine memory and acute recall of details of our family history and former neighborhood.

I'd also like to thank all of those who granted us interviews, memories, and family photos. Because of you, this book has finally come to fruition.

ABOUT AUTHOR AND VISIONARY

Dr. Logan H. Westbrooks

Logan H. Westbrooks was born and raised in Memphis, Tennessee. After graduating from Booker T. Washington High School, he attended LeMoyne-Owen College on a two-year Improved Benevolent Protective Order of Elks of the World (IBPOEW) scholarship. He then transferred to Lincoln University in Jefferson City, Missouri where he earned his B. A in business administration. He was a member of the Lincoln Student Government Association, where he developed his business savvy as a student representative for the Phillip Morris Corporation. He spent two years in the military and later settled in Chicago, Illinois in 1963, where he was hired as a merchandising salesman for Johnson Publishing Company. In 1965 he was hired as a management trainee at RCA/Victor Distributing Corporation in Des Plains, Illinois. Doors of opportunity opened up for him to work in the record division of the company promoting their famous recording artists Sam Cooke and Elvis Presley, while learning the business of selling recorded music.

In 1968, he became the first Black territory salesman at Capitol Records and then he was promoted to regional promotion manager for the Midwest. After two years, Westbrooks was promoted to the position of assistant to the vice president of Marketing and was transferred to the home office of Capitol Records in Hollywood, California.

With each new plateau, Westbrooks leveraged opportunities to merge business with the community. In 1971, he enlisted Capitol Records to contribute financially to the Mafundi Institute; an organization based in Watts, California, that exposed youth to acting and the arts. Westbrooks also implemented a plan with the National Medical Association that more than doubled enrollment for African American students in Medical School by the year 1975.

He also nurtured his relationship with Minette's One Stop, The Leaners, George Daniels' Record Store, Gardner's One Stop, and Rose Book Store and Handleman from his territory salesman days. He left Capitol Records and was subsequently named The National R&B Promotions Director for Mercury Records in Chicago, where he handled releases for artists such as Jerry Butler, Gene Chandler, Melba Moore, Erroll Garner, Buddy Miles, and Rod Stewart.

In November 1971, Westbrooks was hired by music icon Clive Davis to become the first director of Special Markets for CBS Records—a newly created division to penetrate the Black consumer market. He spearheaded efforts to market R&B hits like "Back Stabbers" by the O'Jays and "Me and Mrs. Jones" by Billy Paul. He also worked with artists like Miles Davis, Herbie Hancock, Johnny Mathis, Johnny Nash, the Isley Brothers, Patti Labelle, Taj Mahal, Earth, Wind & Fire, Sly Stone, Modern Jazz Quartet (MJQ), Santana, and many others. He was also the co-architect of a study commissioned by Harvard University about the impact of Black music. The study is called The Harvard Report, and it became a template for Black music marketing divisions. This also spawned another book titled *Power 101: The Harvard Report, Soul Music, and The American Dream*.

In 1976 Logan left CBS Records to join Don Cornelius for the formation of Soul Train Records as vice president of Marketing, in a partnership with Cornelius and Griffey Entertainment. In addition to numerous business ventures, Westbrooks served as a professor at California State University, where he taught two classes: *The Anatomy of a Record Company* and *The Quincy Jones Workshop*, which included Stage Production and Television. More than four hundred students were able to take advantage of this hands-on course of study. Westbrooks also made sure that the class was opened to young people in the neighborhood who were not enrolled at the university.

Additionally, Westbrooks authored the book *The Anatomy of a Record Company*, which he used as a textbook. Westbrooks has contributed to three other publications: *Freedom*, *COGIC: What It Means to Me*, and *Family Affair: Deconstructing the African American Identity*. Dr. Westbrooks' lecture series emphasized the impact and benefits of Historically Black Colleges and Universities (HBCUs) and is often in demand.

In 1972 Logan brought the entire CBS roster of Black artists to Chicago to perform at the Push Expo, along with his entire staff and some volunteers. Also in 1972, he initiated a project to produce a concert for the neighborhood at Mt. Morris Park in Harlem for the neighborhood youngsters with jazz artists as headliners such as Charlie Mingus, Miles Davis, Herbie Hancock, The O'Jays, and Harold Melvin & The Blue Notes.

In 1973 Westbrooks persuaded the Nixon White House to become involved with Black music as a result of his close association with President Nixon's top African American aide Stan Scott. Consequently, as a White House representative, Mr. Scott started attending National Association of Television and Radio Announcers (NATRA) conventions and all-Black music business sessions. Westbrooks persuaded CBS's record division and CBS corporate to underwrite and provide musical acts for Mrs. Coretta Scott King's annual fundraiser at the Omni Coliseum in Atlanta. Westbrooks produced the event which was attended by then governor of Georgia Jimmy Carter and Andrew Young. Through the efforts of Westbrooks, CBS also produced a major gala and fundraiser for the Black Caucus in Washington, DC, with his friend Don Cornelius as emcee, and Nancy Wilson and Isaac Hayes as headliners. As a result of that association, a top African American executive from CBS Records was appointed as a lead fundraiser for the Black Caucus.

In 1974 Westbrooks was appointed by Walter Yetnikoff to spearhead CBS's marketing strategies to explore and capture potential African markets. Westbrooks was then named director of Special Markets for Columbia Records International, as well as managing executive of CBS Records in Africa and Paris, France. He worked there recruiting potential African artists such as Fela Kuti, and to investigate opportunities for Black artists and the recording and manufacturing of records in Nigeria. He also collaborated with Johnny Sekka in planning and implementing the first Jackson 5 African tour in 1974 in Senegal. In doing so, he became the link between the US and Africa, resulting in special associations with Dr. Léopold Sédar Senghor, president of Senegal, and his successor Abdou Diouf. This association led to an appointment as Ambassador for Africa for the Annual African Music Festival for Education in Senegal in 1997.

Residual benefits from his career extended to other aspects of the music business. Westbrooks opened the door for African American promoters who had been blocked access to major artists. Through Westbrooks, Dick Griffey, Al Haymon, and, significantly, Quintin Perry launched successful careers by producing major concerts with Westbrooks' artists at CBS. Westbrooks recognized the importance of Black radio and Black media for editorial content in the entertainment section, and he made a commitment for major advertising dollars for Jet, Essence, and Soul magazines and local Black newspapers in an effort to reach the African American consumer. He also utilized local disk jockeys for radio voiceovers in their markets.

Westbrooks' next endeavor was founding Source Records, which was distributed by MCA Incorporated. Source Records became the home of Chuck Brown & The Soul Searchers, Sharon Paige, Harold Melvin & The Blue Notes, and the group Smash (which was comprised of the DeBarge family). The label created a string of hits that were certified Gold, including the chart-topping "Bustin' Loose," recorded by the late great Godfather of Go-Go Music, Chuck Brown. "Bustin' Loose" also provided the catchy rhythm track for Nelly, who customized his version in 2002 under the title "Hot in Herre" which shot to #1 on Billboard's Top 100 and was certified Double Platinum. Westbrooks was also instrumental in helping African American artists to achieve sales unheard of in the music industry.

Westbrooks has always been committed to community involvement. During a stellar career that has spanned more than fifty years, he has leveraged his business and marketing prowess at his real estate investment firm Westbrooks Management. He and his wife Geri purchased numerous properties in Los Angeles, including the former home of heavyweight champion Jack Dempsey. They converted it into The Helping Hands Home for Boys, which they operated for over fifteen years. The Westbrooks are also former proprietors of Westbrooks Village and the Crenshaw Square shopping mall, where they made famous the Sunny Sunday Arts show, a hub for local artists to convene and sell their wares.

Westbrooks was ordained in 1996 by the Church of God in Christ and received his master's in biblical counseling from Eternal Word Graduate School. His dedication to the Church of God in Christ's mission to broaden and strengthen the territory of their churches in Monrovia and Azusa, California, resulted in increased numbers coming to Christ and additional services to those in need. Currently he serves as executive secretary of the Metropolitan Ecclesiastical Jurisdiction of Southern California and administrative assistant to the jurisdictional bishop.

Westbrooks has been interviewed or chronicled by local and national press, as well as PBS and the BBC. Highlights of his career have been enshrined in the Logan H. Westbrooks Collection at Indiana University's Archives of African American Music and Culture, which is also available online at *http://www.indiana.edu/~aamc/*. In 2014 the ultimate honor was bestowed when LeMoyne-Owen College in Memphis, Tennessee, conferred upon Logan Westbrooks an honorary doctorate of humane letters.

Among his many affiliations, Westbrooks is a lifetime member of the National Association for the Advancement of Colored People (NAACP) and Omega Psi Phi Fraternity. Dr. Westbrooks was also a 2008 Lincoln University Distinguished Alumni and an inductee in the 2009 Historically Black Colleges and Universities (HBCU) Alumni Hall of Fame. As a video producer he has developed *It's Never Too Late, The Healing House, Home of the Heroes, Your Hollywood Local, Step by Step @ LA*, and *Freedom's Pathway Forward*.

Adding to a long list of commendations, Westbrooks has been named to receive the 2015 Faith Award from Faith Love & Hope Unlimited, The Music Pioneer Award from United Music Heritage, Inc., and The Vanguard Award from the Living Legends Foundation. Currently Westbrooks celebrates the release of five books: *Anatomy of a Record Company 1 & 2, The Anatomy of the Music Industry: How the Game Was & How the Game Has Changed, The Harvard Report: Censored, Power 101* (with Schuyler Traughber) and *Lauderdale Sub*. All are published by Ascent Books and available on Amazon and at *LoganWestbrooks.com*.

Countless people have benefitted from his career because of his concern for community and society at large. With each phase of his life, he felt a responsibility and a sense of duty to share the knowledge and insight he learned as a result of his position. Rather than separating himself, he always sought to pull others into the fold by developing ideas and creating civic and business opportunities to move people forward.

Dr. Logan H. Westbrooks will forever be a global legend and trailblazer who helped shape Black music in every form. He redefined marketing Black music and African American artists and became the first African American music executive to have such a distinguished career at major record labels. His pioneering work of paving the way for African American executives and artists in the music industry has left a legacy of artists and music yet to be heard.

Dr. Westbrooks and his lovely wife Geri enjoy dual residences in Sherman Oaks, California, and Memphis, Tennessee. He is the proud father of Babette Moxey, who married Jeremy Moxey, grandfather to Brienne, Jordan, Elliott, and Emelia Hart, and great-grandfather to Arthur Hodgetts.

CONTENTS

Message from the Editor 8

Special Thanks 11

About Author and Visionary 12

Introduction 23

Overview of the Neighborhood 25

The Bishop Family 36

The Bryant Family 41

The Davenport Family 45

The Haley Family 55

The Hawkins Porter Smith Family 58

The Hodges Family 72

The Moore Family 80

The Neely Family 89

The Patterson Family 103

The Stiles Katoe Family 116

The Weaver Howard Family 120

The Westbrooks Family 135

Reginald Smith & The Family Day Care 162

Reflections from Logan H. Westbrooks	170
Carnegie Church of God in Christ	187
Morning View Baptist Church	191
Mt. Sinai Missionary Baptist Church	195
Reflections	199
Reversal of Fortune	219
Family Photo Gallery	228
Lauderdale Sub Photo Gallery	281
Index	290

INTRODUCTION

I have been blessed to have a career in which I traveled the world. However, each time I visit Memphis, I am reminded of my humble beginnings in a part of town called the Lauderdale Subdivision, affectionately known as Lauderdale Sub.

This book is a tribute to those days and those families, whom I vividly remember. They resided in the Lauderdale Sub from about the 1940s to the 1960s, and in some cases on up until the present time.

My initial objective was to interview all of the twenty-five families that came to mind. Once we began, it was clear that too much time had transpired in order to secure a direct line of communication to them or their descendants. In most cases the matriarchs and patriarchs had passed on, as well as their offspring. They were my friends, classmates, and mentors.

Just for my own sake, here's the complete list that we hoped to represent in this book: The Anderson Family, The Bishop Family, The Bobo Family, The Bradford Family, The Brown Family, The Bryant Family, The Dandridge Family, The Davenport Family, The Doggett Family, The Gilliam Family, The Haley Family, The Hawkins Porter Smith Family, The Hodges Family, The Givens Family, The Suggs Family, The Holman Family, The Johnson Family, The London Family, The Matthews Family,

The Humphrey Moore Family, The Warren Moore Family, The Neely Family, The Oliver Family, The Patterson Family, The Stiles Family, The Thomas Family, The Weaver Family, The Woods Family, The Yates Family, The Young Family, and of course my family, The Westbrooks.

I have been blessed to have an immaculate memory in my senior years. Being a man of great ambition, I anticipated that we'd be able to reach someone from every family, alive, well and willing to share their family stories from the designated era for this book. Actually, I waited until 2023 to even begin this project. So many connections have been lost. Nearly all of the families have moved away and today the neighborhood known as the Lauderdale Sub is mostly blighted.

Undeterred, we pursued all of the families. While we did not reach someone from every family on the list, we count it a blessing to have amassed more than a dozen interviews from some of the families listed above. In most cases it was the children or grandchildren of the matriarchs and patriarchs that I remember as a young man.

This book captures a rare treasure and a chance to pique the recollection of a dozen individuals (including me) who share their memories and success stories as a result of Lauderdale Sub.

Within their stories is a through line to several of the other families with whom we did not connect personally, but all in all it gives a clear picture of the nobility of this great community.

CHAPTER 1

OVERVIEW OF THE NEIGHBORHOOD

Memories of the neighborhood from Dr. Logan H. Westbrooks

Lauderdale Sub is located in South Memphis. It is bordered on the north by Parkway and on the south by Person Street. It is bordered on the east by Victor and on the west by Lauderdale. At Lauderdale and Waldorf, it goes further west to Latham Street and south of Waldorf to Person Street.

It consists of the following streets from west to east: Lauderdale, Carnegie, McMillan, Ely, Miller, Orleans, Gabby, Webb, and Victor streets. From north to south, the streets are Waldorf, Essex, and Person.

At Lauderdale and Waldorf, west to Latham, those streets are Humber, Person, South Wellington, Shadowlawn, Camaron, Preston, and Latham.

This book focuses on the years 1945 to 1961 and highlights the families that lived there then.

LAUDERDALE SUB: MEMORIES OF A MEMPHIS NEIGHBORHOOD

Families in Lauderdale Sub mostly consisted of a mother and father in each household and an average of four children.

The patriarch was the head of the household and labored outside of the home, and the matriarch was a housewife.

There were several schoolteachers, two postal workers, one medical doctor, business owners, auto mechanics, a trucking company, hairdressers, and several ministers.

The neighborhood consisted of Morning View Missionary Baptist Church (1626 Carnegie), Greater Mount Nebo Baptist Church (1608 Ely), Mt. Sinai Baptist Church (1667 S. Lauderdale), Harris Memorial Christian Methodist Episcopal Church (1572 S. Lauderdale), and Carnegie Church of God in Christ (1584 Carnegie Street).

Dr. Logan H. Westbrooks

CHAPTER 1: OVERVIEW OF THE NEIGHBORHOOD

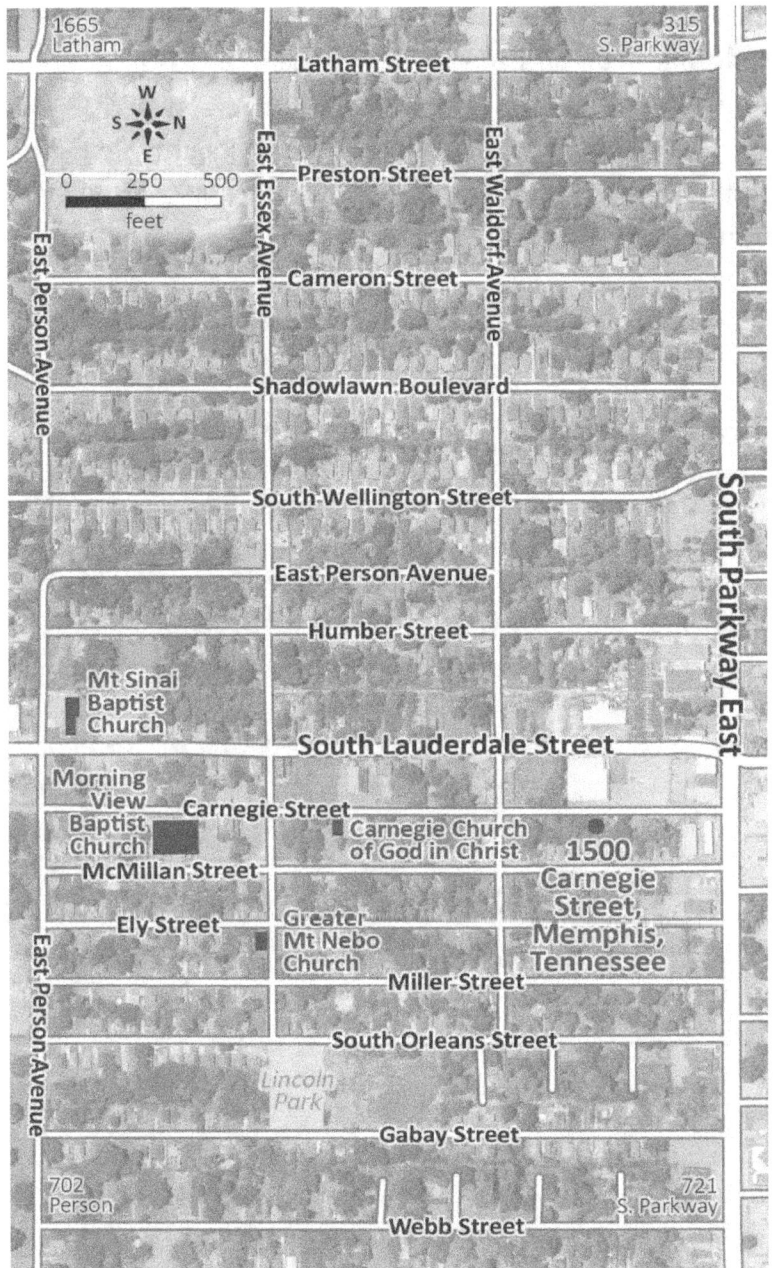

Map of Lauderdale Sub

It consisted of two grocery stores. Chambers was located at Waldorf and McMillan. Then there was a drug store at Lauderdale and Parkway, a five-and-dime shop on Parkway and Lauderdale, a White-owned café at Carnegie and Parkway, a donut shop at Parkway and Carnegie, a furniture store at Parkway and Carnegie, a dry cleaner at Lauderdale and Waldorf, a juke joint at Parkway, a sundry store at Essex and Orleans Street, and another sundry at Lauderdale and Essex.

Lincoln Elementary School was for grades one through eight. It was located at 1566 Orleans Street.

There were only a few families who owned automobiles.

Public transportation was by the #4 Lauderdale bus that went all the way to downtown Memphis. All of the streets were paved.

My family moved to 1500 Carnegie Street in the summer of 1945, and I enrolled in the fourth grade at Lincoln Elementary School in September.

My family consisted of my brother Alphonso, who was two years older than me, my older sister Shirley, my sister Pearl, and my youngest sister Gloria.

Prior to moving to the Lauderdale Sub, our home church was The Temple Church of God in Christ, pastored by Bishop Charles Harrison Mason. When we moved to Lauderdale Sub our membership was transferred to the Carnegie Church of God in Christ, pastored by Elder Samuel McNeal Sr.

When we moved from Lauderdale Sub to 1045 Latham Street, our family transferred back to the Temple Church of God in Christ.

During the era, everything in Memphis was segregated. The closest park was Lincoln Park near Bunker Hill and Hamilton School, which was less than a mile away. It seemed much further when we were kids.

CHAPTER 1: OVERVIEW OF THE NEIGHBORHOOD

The closest theater for Blacks (which were referred to as Colored at the time) was The Ace Theater on Mississippi and Walker Avenue. The next was The Georgia Theater on Georgia Avenue and Lauderdale. Then from there we'd go to The New Daisy, The Old Daisy, and The Palace, which were on Beale Street.

There was also The Malco and The Pantages Theater on Main Street where Coloreds were only allowed to sit in the balcony. The Royal #2 was a White theater at 1320 Lauderdale. It later became Willie Mitchell Studios, where legendary recordings were made by Al Green, O. V. Wright, Donald Bryant, and Ann Peebles. In recent years Bruno Mars and The Hooligans recorded there. Among the featured musicians was Memphian Kameron Whalum III on trumpet and backgrounds.

All churches were segregated. There were Colored water fountains in department stores. Colored people could not try on clothes in department stores. At the service stations they had one toilet designated for Colored male and females. There was no public library or museum for Colored people.

Our nearest Colored High School was Booker T. Washington and that was two miles away, and we walked to school rain or shine.

There were a few Lauderdale Sub students that went to Saint Augustine Catholic School, which was a mile and a half away. There were a few other families that sent their children to Hamilton High School, instead of Booker T. Washington.

The closest family to our home on Carnegie who gained notoriety was the Brown family. They lived two doors down from us. Garnett Brown became a renowned trombone player that eventually played with Herbie Hancock, Earth, Wind & Fire, Lionel Richie, and more. He had an illustrious music career. He had two sisters and a brother named Samuel. His younger sister Margaret attended Meharry Medical College in Nashville, Tennessee and became a dental hygienist. His other sister Jean attended LeMoyne-Owen College, and she was a part of the LeMoyne Eight who staged a historic sit-in during the civil rights era.

The next closest family to our home on Carnegie was the Styles family who lived on McMillan behind us. We will learn about them in their own chapter in the book.

The next closest family that lived near me and my siblings was the Davenport family. The father was Herbert Davenport Sr. The mother was Addie Westbrook Davenport. Dr. Herbert Eugene Davenport Jr. was a former student at Booker T., and he also became the pastor of Friendship Baptist Church in Shell Lake, Arkansas, and Shiloh Baptist Church in Memphis. Herbert Jr. had a section of Person Street named after him in Lauderdale Sub in 2015. More on the Davenport family is also featured in the book.

The next closest family was the Dandridge family. Their father worked on the railroad, and their mother was a housewife. They lived on Carnegie, next door to Morning View Baptist Church. The brother and sister went to Lincoln Elementary and then on to Booker T. Washington High School. The sibling Eddie Dandridge was my age, and he was my classmate. Eddie became a local prominent musician and keyboardist. He formed a band that was very popular and prominent in the Mid-South area.

Also, on this same block of Carnegie was the Johnson family. The older brother L. C. was the same age as my brother Alphonso. L. C., the younger brother, and sister all attended Booker T. Washington. L. C. joined the Peace Corps after college. I have fond memories of Carnegie Street and the surrounding streets in the neighborhood.

CHAPTER 1: OVERVIEW OF THE NEIGHBORHOOD

Humphrey Moore Jr. RIP. July 20, 2020

James Neely and wife Barbara, Peggy White, Logan Westbrooks—Booker T. Washington High School Reunion

I remember the family of Humphrey Moore Sr. My playmate and classmate was Humphrey Jr. His brother Peter went to Tennessee State and became a pilot for American Airlines. The Neely family lived on Lauderdale Street. The matriarch of the family was a housewife. Once all of her children finished school, she eventually became a nurse. The father owned several trucks and a trucking business. His trucks hauled building materials. He hired a lot of men from the neighborhood.

James Neely was my age, my classmate, and my childhood friend. We sold newspapers together for the *Memphis World*. He became a mogul in the BBQ industry and put Interstate BBQ on the map.

Also on Lauderdale Street was the Yates family. Clifford was the oldest son, and he was also my classmate. I remember he had a sister named Nadine.

Lauderdale Street was also home to the Bishop family. The father was a postal worker, and the mother was a schoolteacher.

I sold the *Memphis World* newspaper with the Bishop family, Jessie and Jimmy Bishop, as well as James Neely. There are so many vivid memories of the people who lived, worked, worshiped, and were cultivated in this Lauderdale Sub community. To look at it today, you could not imagine the greatness that came out of this neighborhood and the far-reaching impact.

I am a businessman, entrepreneur, record company executive, author, real estate investor, world traveler, college professor, child advocate, dedicated husband, family man, and a proud former pastor. This is a direct result of my life in the Church of God in Christ.

The founder was Bishop C. H. Mason, who presided from 1897 to 1961. Several bishops served under his leadership and his legacy. Among them are Bishop O. T. Jones (1962–1968), Bishop J. O. Patterson (1968–1989), Bishop Louis S. Ford (1990–1995), Bishop Chandler Owens

CHAPTER 1: OVERVIEW OF THE NEIGHBORHOOD

(1995–2000), and my childhood friend in Lauderdale Sub, Gilbert Earl Patterson who presided from 2000 to 2007. Bishop Charles S. Blake was presiding bishop from 2007 to 2021 and now Bishop Drew Sheard is the presiding bishop as of 2021.

Bishop C. H. Mason

Al Westbrooks Jr. working for Bishop Ford at Mason Temple in 1952

I also saw the rise of my brother Alphonso Westbrooks Jr. from working with Bishop Ford in Public Relations for the church and eventually becoming the national director of Public Relations for the Church of God in Christ.

Alphonso earned an undergraduate degree in journalism from Lincoln University in Jefferson City, Missouri, and a master's in mass communications from the University of Chicago. The highlight of his career with Church of God in Christ (COGIC) was when he directed all press and publicity for the visit of former President Bill Clinton for his visit to Mason Temple in 1993. He was a proud product of Lauderdale Sub. I also witnessed my sister Pearl leading the opening song "It Is Well" with the Tennessee Mass Choir at Bishop Mason's homegoing. She is also a product of Lauderdale Sub.

Nowadays when driving through Lauderdale Sub with my two nephews, I am saddened at the condition of the once thriving neighborhood with children laughing and playing and parents interacting with each other and looking after everybody's children.

A flood of memories instantly overtook me, such as happily walking to school with my playmates, being at the corner of Parkway and Carnegie walking to the store, going to the candy store and the donut shop on Parkway.

There were so many contented and happy families. Back then we attended each other's birthday parties and interacted at our local church, Carnegie COGIC, Sunday School, Young People Willing Workers (YPWW), Vacation Bible School, all day church services and revivals.

There were memories of raising pet rabbits and swapping them with James and Harry Neely. I have memories of my pet goat and building a cart for the goat to pull with my sister Gloria riding in the cart. There were so many happy times.

CHAPTER 1: OVERVIEW OF THE NEIGHBORHOOD

Let's yield to a few of the families that we were able to speak with firsthand to recall their family history and memories of Lauderdale Sub.

Young Logan Westbrooks with his pet goat

CHAPTER 2

THE BISHOP FAMILY

*Memories of the Bishop family from
Dr. James Bishop*

Dr. James J. Bishop, chairman of the National Annual Fund Campaign, considers the generosity of the LeMoyne-Owen College alumni pivotal to the college embracing its future. (Courtsey photo)

CHAPTER 2: THE BISHOP FAMILY

When you say Lauderdale, it covers a lot. I am James Joseph Bishop, PhD. My doctorate degree is in inorganic chemistry. My PhD is from MIT, and my undergraduate degree is from LeMoyne, which is now LeMoyne-Owen College as of 1958.

I finished high school at Booker T. Washington 1954. I attended Lincoln Elementary. My mother's name is Memory Austin Bishop and my father's name is Jesse Henry Joseph Bishop Sr. My mother also spent time in Lauderdale Sub. She grew up in the house next door to where we are today, which is my father's house. My father did not live in the neighborhood until after they were married.

Mother left Pontotoc, Mississippi as a young woman. There were no high schools there for Black people. She came to Memphis and attended what was then LeMoyne Normal School, where she got a degree, and she stayed for part of that time at 1616 Lauderdale Street.

I can't exactly recall when my mother came to Memphis, but it would have been right after high school. She was born in 1903 so she probably came to Memphis around 1920.

My father grew up in Natchez, Mississippi. I'm not sure what year he came to Memphis. He and my mother met through some other people from Memphis. They got married around 1929 or 1930.

My oldest sibling is my late sister Memory Kathryn Bishop Wills. That was her last name when she died. My brother was Jesse Henry Bishop Jr. I only had one sister and one brother.

As for school, I go all the way back Miss Potts' Kindergarten up on Mississippi Boulevard. She was very religious. This was before I went to Lincoln Elementary, then Booker T. Washington High School and on to LeMoyne.

My father was a postman in Memphis. One year he got sick and then my mother did some domestic work. Then she became a substitute teacher before advancing to be a regular teacher in the Memphis schools. She taught for fourth grade for decades at Florida Street School. My mother's aunt was Mamie Kate Jackson. She and her husband Moses Jackson built a home in Lauderdale Sub. This was the house in which we lived at 1622 South Lauderdale.

The Bishop family home at 1616 Lauderdale St.

My mother's grandparents were in Lauderdale Sub around the turn of the nineteenth century. This would have been the very early 1900s. However, my grandparents lived in North Memphis.

My parents always told us to keep going with our education. So, how did we do it? It was because they gave us hope. I knew very early in life that I had to go to college. My aunt and my grandparents put a lot of money in the bank. It wasn't enough to pay for college, but it was certainly an incentive.

CHAPTER 2: THE BISHOP FAMILY

Our teachers at Lincoln, Booker T. Washington High School, and LeMoyne-Owen College told us what brought on segregation, Jim Crow, and economic discrimination. We needed to progress intellectually, economically, politically, physically, spiritually, and organizationally to defeat it and we're still doing that. It's not over yet.

The churches were very important in our neighborhoods. Sunday School taught us how to read and how to talk and how to give speeches at Easter. That's an important part of becoming an active citizen. That's an important part of our neighborhood.

There was a woman named Mrs. Sherman who lived in the 1600 block of Carnegie. She had her own beauty shop in her home. She also had a Coca Cola machine, and I think she had the first television in our neighborhood. Mrs. Sherman would turn her TV around in the window at night and we could sit out in the yard and watch it.

She also had a son who had a mental issue. So, it was very nice that he got a chance to watch TV with children of his own age. Actually, we all got a chance to watch TV, because we couldn't afford our own.

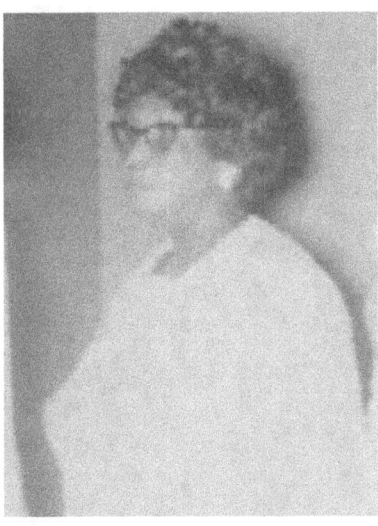

Mrs. Sherman from Carnegie Street
(Photo: Courtesy of LaRita Shelby, circa 1977)

Mrs. Sherman may have had the first air conditioners. Her home was always cool. She was a thriving entrepreneur, a businesswoman who fixed hair and sold Coca Cola. She was a major part of the neighborhood.

I left Memphis in 1958 and went off to graduate school. Dr. James Bishop was a 2020 Hall of Fame honoree for the Tennessee Independent Colleges and Universities Association. He was instrumental in founding an innovative program at Ohio State University in 1988 to increase the number of Black, Hispanic, and other underrepresented minority scholars from low-income families who wanted to attend four-year colleges and universities. He also served as an interim president at LeMoyne-Owen College.

CHAPTER 3

THE BRYANT FAMILY

*Memories of The Bryant Family from
Beatrice Bryant Terry*

I am Beatrice Bryant Terry. I grew up in Carnegie Church of God in Christ. Bryant is my maiden name. I have two sisters and seven brothers. Our address was 1629 Cameron Street.

We lived there all of our lives. The family house was there all of our lives. I'd say we lived there from the 1930s through 2022.

*Mr. & Mrs. Edward and Margie Bryant Sr.
Photo courtesy of the Bryant family*

My father and mother were Edward Bryant Sr. and Margie Bryant. The sisters are Tina, Beatrice, and Brenda. Tina is an educator who taught for about thirty years and I (Beatrice Bryant Terry) became a nurse. Brenda worked at Shelby State College.

The Bryant family is also very proud of ten children. There were three sisters and seven brothers, one of which is Donald Bryant, a singer well known in Memphis and worldwide.

Songwriter & Entertainer Donald Bryant. Photo: Discogs

The brothers are Elon, Edward Jr., Jamie, Gene, Donald, Kenneth, and Charles Gene, better known as "Rat," was an auto mechanic and helped people out in the neighborhood. Everybody in the neighborhood knew him as "Rat." The other brothers worked at various jobs wherever they could find work.

We were a close-knit family. We were a church going family. We were a singing family. Just about everybody in the family sang. A couple of my brothers were in a singing group that sang locally in Memphis.

CHAPTER 3: THE BRYANT FAMILY

As for the neighborhood, you know, it wasn't just one mother, your house mother, but all the ladies up and down the street were your mother. If you were caught doing something, they disciplined you just like you were their child. They looked out for each other and their children.

The family church was the Carnegie Church of God and Christ. We went on Sundays, practically all day. Then we went sometimes in the evening during the week. We had Bible Study and Willing Workers. I guess that's all I can remember.

As far as education is concerned, all of the children in the family went to Lincoln Elementary, Lincoln Junior High, and Booker T. Washington High School. Some of us went to Memphis State, Shelby State College, and LeMoyne-Owen College.

Our family was aware of the turbulent times in the country, but we just believed that things were getting better. We believed in our faith and that it would bring us through. The year that Martin Luther King Jr. was killed in 1968 was a bad time for Memphis, and especially a bad time for me because that was my senior year. We didn't get have a prom due to the death of Dr. King, and going to the prom was a big thing.

There was violence throughout the city. It was terrible. My mother and father were still alive at that time. They were telling us to stay at home and don't leave the yard. You know, we had to be vigilant because so much was happening during that time.

We all managed to be successful despite it all. My brother Donald is a well-known musician. He's married to blues singer Ann Peebles and he's still singing. He was just recently inducted into the Memphis Blues Hall of Fame.

The family group was named The Four Kings, that was their name. As for my other siblings, my brother Charles had his own business. He was a painter.

The best part of living in that community and knowing everybody in the neighborhood and far beyond our neighborhood, is that people were friendly back then. They cared for each other. Everybody knew everybody and not just two or three streets over. We knew each other a long ways off.

The Four Kings. Photo: Discogs

CHAPTER 4

THE DAVENPORT FAMILY

Memories of The Davenport family from Magnolia "Sweet Baby" Davenport Matthews

Magnolia Davenport Matthews

I lived my entire childhood at 1563 McMillan. My parents were Addie Westbrook Davenport and Herbert Davenport Sr. Of course, I'm not the oldest child that lived there, but my older siblings lived at the same address.

I never knew my grandmother, but my oldest sister did. My dad's mom lived there. Her name was Virginia Hawkins Davenport. My older sister was born there in 1934. So, she lived there at that same address. I can't really say when they actually moved to that address.

Virginia Davenport was indeed a "Hawkins" before she became a "Davenport." As far as her siblings, the only one that I knew was Uncle Bud (Walter Hawkins Sr.).

During the Depression Era, the Hawkins family was living in Athens, Georgia, and their home burned down. My grandmother (Virginia Hawkins Davenport) invited her brother Walter, his wife, and children to come to Memphis and live with her. That's how they ended up in Memphis.

Walter Guy Hawkins Sr. and Willie G. Hawkins relocated to Memphis with seven of their nine children, as I recall. I only knew seven of them when they moved from Athens, Georgia, to Memphis.

Two other Hawkins' sons, Lord Kelvin and Howard Hawkins, did not live with the family in Memphis. Howard is said to have gone off to war, and when he came back, he had lost his mind. He went off one day and never returned. I didn't know Lord Kelvin but was told there was some encounter where he was killed. Either he was a taxi driver and he got stabbed and died on the road, or he died because no one would help him or something like that. That had to have happened before they moved to Memphis.

The seven that we do know of first came to 1563 McMillan. They were Ritta, Claudia, Susie, Walter Jr., Marylou, Florence, and Floretta. These were my cousins. So now we have two large families at 1563 McMillan Street.

CHAPTER 4: THE DAVENPORT FAMILY

They had moved out of that address before I was born. In fact, it's my understanding that when they moved to Memphis, they didn't stay at that address very long before they moved out.

The next house that my Uncle Bud (Walter Hawkins) bought was right around the corner at 1658 Carnegie Street. I think they moved to another house before they moved to Carnegie Street.

My grandmother Virginia Davenport was married to my grandfather Jake Davenport. He was already dead before I was born. Apparently, my older siblings Ann, Herbert Jr., and Hattie remembered my grandmother. My siblings Hattie Marie, Herbert Jr., and Roy (my younger brother) have since passed away.

Herbert Jr., Virginia Hawkins Davenport, seated Arnice, and standing Ann Katherine Davenport

1563 McMillan Street was the original house of Virginia Hawkins Davenport and Jake Davenport. Their children Herbert Davenport Sr.

and Magnolia Davenport (later married name Howard) were born there. I was named after my Aunt Magnolia, my father's sister.

Apparently, they had a half-sister, but I don't remember her name. I think she died before any of us were born so we really didn't know her. We only knew the two children of Jake and Virginia Davenport, and they were my dad (Herbert Sr.), and my Aunt Magnolia.

The Davenport family: Hattie, Magnolia, Herbert Sr., Roneta, Ann Katherine, Arnice, and Herbert Jr.
Not pictured Addie and Roy.

The Davenports are Herbert Sr. and Addie Westbrook Davenport.

Their children are Annie Catherine, Herbert Jr., Addie Arnice, Hattie Marie, Magnolia (Sweet Baby), Roneta, and Roy Davenport. They are descendants of Virginia Hawkins Davenport, the sister of Walter Guy Hawkins. This piece connects the Hawkins, the Davenport, the Howard, and the Weaver families.

CHAPTER 4: THE DAVENPORT FAMILY

Addie Westbrook Davenport

A man named Simon Howard came into play at some point. The first Magnolia Davenport (my aunt) married Simon Howard sometime around 1920. This union made her Magnolia Davenport Howard.

They became the parents of Claribelle Howard, Emma Dee Howard, Clarence Howard, and Simon Howard Jr. We called him Pop. I don't recall what Virginia Hawkins Davenport and Jake Davenport did for a living. My dad, Herbert Sr., was a Pullman Porter before he had a tumor in his leg. He ended up having one of his legs amputated. So that's when he became a barber.

I think Virginia may have worked as a domestic. From my understanding, she was also involved in the Church of God in Christ. If she was walking down the street and saw someone doing something wrong, she would say: "Loose them Satan!" This is according to my oldest sister Ann.

What we do know is that our family has a legacy of faith, education, community service, and achievement. Our immediate family has a legacy in the nursing industry. We have a lot of nurses.

The first nurse was my sister Hattie. She had been a nurse for four or five years and seeing her involvement in nursing inspired me. Then I became a nurse and then my late sister Hattie Marie Davenport Martin's daughter-in-law became a nurse. Not only is she a nurse, but she also has her doctorate in nursing. She is Dr. Judy C. Martin, former chief of Nursing Shelby County, TN.

Her daughter Julia is also a nurse, and she also has her doctorate in nursing (Dr. Julia Martin Steed). My sister Roneta has a daughter who is a nurse, and my oldest sister Ann has a granddaughter who is a nurse. My daughter Judy worked as a secretary in a hospital.

I also want to mention that I have three grandchildren. My oldest grandchild Ashley is an educator. She teaches school and lives in Nashville. My second granddaughter Lauren is an architect. She works for a company called LRK, and my youngest grandson is a firefighter in Marietta, Georgia.

The sons of Herbert Davenport Sr. were my two brothers. Rev. Herbert Davenport Jr. was my pastor at one point. He ministered at Shiloh Baptist Church.

Herbert Jr. was there for 22 years, and he passed away in 2012. I had a younger brother also. In fact, Roy Westbrook Davenport was the youngest of all of us.

Westbrook was my mom's maiden name. Roy was in the armed services (the US Army) from 1970 to 1972. He came back and he became sick.

He was diagnosed with schizophrenia. My sister Hattie took care of him until she passed.

Then I took care of him. He passed in 2014. So those were the only two brothers.

CHAPTER 4: THE DAVENPORT FAMILY

Rev. Dr. Herbert Davenport Jr.

Roy Westbrook Davenport

I was told that my Uncle Bud (Walter Hawkins) was a preacher. I was born and raised up in Morning View Baptist Church. I think Uncle Bud was a Baptist and he was associated with Morning View. My aunt Willie (Hawkins of 1658 Carnegie) was the one who was associated with the Church of God in Christ.

The Westbrooks family were also associated with the Church of God in Christ on Carnegie Street.

My brother Herbert was involved with the young men at Booker T. Washington School. He organized a clothing giveaway among his friends who were also in ministry. He had them to buy suits and ties for young men in the community. He wanted to show them how to be men. His daughter was teaching at Vance Elementary School, and she learned of the need for clothing for young women. She shared this with her father and so Herbert Jr. did the same thing at his daughter's school.

I spoke to a young man recently who was the assistant principal at Lester School. He was talking to my brother one day about how some of the young men needed shoes and didn't have the right clothing to wear, and one day my brother (Rev. Davenport) came to school and had a bag of money and gave it to him. And he said that my brother went to a bunch of his preacher friends and asked them for money.

He did so much. He was the neighborhood preacher. When anybody needed him for anything in the neighborhood, he was always there. So they were working on the street named for him before he passed but they finalized naming Person Street from Elvis Presley Boulevard to Lauderdale Street "Honorary Reverend Herbert E. Davenport Jr. Avenue."

I left Lincoln Elementary in the spring of 1954. So, I started at Booker T. Washington in the fall of 1954. So, the group had to be formulated around 1953, 1954, or 1955. It was named The Memphis Jewels. We sang on several radio stations including WDIA and also in West Memphis on KWAM.

CHAPTER 4: THE DAVENPORT FAMILY

Rev. Herbert E. Davenport Jr. Ave.

Betty Bond, Lillian Hines, Vivian Bond, Magnolia Davenport, unknown teen, & Florence Hawkins

As for other achievements, I was in a group called The Memphis Jewels. They hailed from the Lauderdale Sub. The person that formed this group was none other than Florence Hawkins, mother of LaRita Shelby. Florence started The Memphis Jewels in the early 1950s.

Florence Hawkins was one of the twins that lived at 1658 Carnegie. The twins are Florence and Floretta.

Florence's music teacher was Lucie Campbell, a very famous gospel musician and songwriter who wrote "Something Within," "Touch Me Lord Jesus," "The Kings Highway," "He'll Understand," and "Say Well Done." Florence could play and sing. She was really strict about her group The Memphis Jewels. I mean, we would practice, practice, practice! We were also written up in the newspaper. I'm not sure how that came about. I think it was just her being so serious about our group. We were singing on the radio and like I said, I think it was KWAM in West Memphis, Arkansas.

What I most attribute as being the glue of our family was that we were so close. Family was just that, family. We were close to the Hawkins family. In fact, in 1954 our house (on McMillan) also burned. The Hawkins who had moved to 1658 Carnegie by that time, let us live there until our house was rebuilt.

I believe it was Hattie and I who lived at the Carnegie address and my sister Arnice lived with the Weavers (who were also family members) until our house was rebuilt.

What I am most proud of from my family and the families from the Lauderdale Sub is our closeness. In the Lauderdale Sub everybody knew everybody. It was one of those things. If I were coming down the street, and I was doing something that I shouldn't have done, before I got home whoever saw me would tell my parents before I got home.

It was just such a closeness. I mean, it's just something that was at that time. You didn't think that it was a big deal, but now you miss that.

CHAPTER 5

THE HALEY FAMILY

Memories of the Haley Family from Lizzie Haley, wife of James C. Haley

James C. Haley

I'm Lizzie Haley. I was the wife of James C. Haley. Okay. My connection to the Lauderdale Sub is by marriage only because my husband James grew up in the Lauderdale Sub as part of the Haley family.

The patriarch of the Haley family was JC. I'm not sure what the JC stood for. It had JC in the obituary. My husband's mother was Corinne Haley, and they were from Lauderdale Sub.

My husband would have been eighty-one years old at the time of this interview, and his sibling was named Gloria. I was married to James. It was just the two of them. James had children, but his children never lived in Lauderdale Sub.

James worked at Firestone during the summertime and after school was out at LeMoyne. James was also a middle school science teacher at Havenview School here in Memphis. His daddy did odd jobs in the neighborhood, and he worked at Firestone. James worked at Firestone only temporarily, and I think that his sister Gloria worked there for a short time.

The family church home was Morning View. They started out at Morning View and his mom, sister, and James transferred to Centenary United Methodist Church. His mom and Gloria stayed there for some period of time and left. James' church home was Centenary United Methodist before he passed. They were Jehovah's Witnesses. Gloria is still living, and their mom is deceased.

James attended Lincoln Elementary, and he graduated from Hamilton High. He said that his mom would not let him go to Booker T. She was having him go to Hamilton, where some of his cousins were. I don't know whether she was comparing schools or not, but he could have gone to either. It was his mom's decision for him to go to Hamilton.

As far as some beautiful memories of the Haley family values are concerned, I can simply say that they were all avid church goers. Even

CHAPTER 5: THE HALEY FAMILY

though James went to seminary, his mom went to the (Kingdom) hall as well as his sister, but they were all involved in the church. They helped other people. They visited the sick and shut-ins, and they participated in certain programs and committees and all of that.

James enjoyed photography and he took many pictures. As a matter of fact, he had an afterschool photography class where he taught free of charge. It was one of his activities and one of his passions. James' mom was a double amputee. I don't know if that's important information for you, but she lived to be one hundred years old. That's basically all I know.

He had cousins though and some of them may remember more than I do. Although James took a lot of pictures, the ones that I have are pictures of James' family when we get married, and that was like twenty-plus years ago. Okay, I'm not talking about what happened in 1946. His first wife died in 1965, and we married in 2001. So, I don't have those pictures. I have a picture of his family from the 2000s.

The name of people that really have information that's pertinent to what you're doing are Alfred Mitchell and Lawrence Haley. Vivian Louise Malone Wesson lived on Miller Street, and those other two are James' first cousins. Their daddies are brothers, and James Haley's dad was their daddy's brother.

CHAPTER 6

THE HAWKINS PORTER SMITH FAMILY

Memories of the Hawkins Porter Smith Family from Dr. Reginald Porter Sr. who shared this prior to his passing December 24, 2024.

Dr. Reginald L. Porter Sr.

I am Rev. Dr. Reginald L. Porter Sr. Just recently, I retired as the pastor of Metropolitan Baptist Church. Currently, I am pastor emeritus. I am formerly pastor of Saint John Number One Baptist Church in Jackson, Tennessee, and Greenwood Baptist Church in Tuskegee, Alabama.

I'm not exactly sure of the dates and years, but the Hawkins family (at least my grandfather and grandmother Walter Guy and Willie G. Hawkins), along with my mother (Ritta Hawkins Porter Smith) moved to the Lauderdale Sub somewhere in the 1930s and they lived in the home on McMillan Street. Later, my grandfather and grandmother purchased the house at 1658 Carnegie Street and then my mother remarried and we moved to 1671 McMillan Street. So, I grew up at 1658 Carnegie Street and 1671 McMillan.

Reginald Porter Sr., Ritta Hawkins Porter (Smith) and Roderick Porter Sr. on the steps of 1658 Carnegie.

I cannot remember the address specifically, but my grandfather Walter G. Hawkins and my grandmother Willie G. Hawkins came to Memphis from Athens, Georgia, to live with his sister and her husband, that's

Herbert Davenport Sr. and Virginia Davenport. They all lived together on McMillan Street. Later on, Walter Hawkins (my grandfather) and Willie G. Hawkins (my grandmother) moved with their family to 1658 Carnegie Street.

My mother later remarried. My mother Ritta married Stanie Smith, Sr. and they lived at 1671 McMillan Street. So, I grew up between those two addresses.

Herbert Davenport Sr. was the husband of Virginia Hawkins Davenport and Herbert Davenport Jr. was their son. Virginia Hawkins Davenport was the sister of Walter Hawkins, my grandfather.

The family members that lived at 1658 Carnegie in the Lauderdale Sub at this time was my mother Ritta, my Aunt Claudia, my Aunt Mary, my aunt Susie, my twin aunts Floretta and Florence, and my Uncle Walter Jr.

Lord Kelvin Hawkins passed away in Georgia, and Howard Hawkins would have moved with the family and lived at 1658 Carnegie. From what I was told, Howard had gone done time in the service. Based on it, I do not remember whether it was World War II or the Korean War and I'm not sure of the circumstances, but he had shell shock of some kind. I remember as a child, I knew him briefly on Carnegie Street, but he was having an aftereffect from the war. I wouldn't say that he lost his mind. He was suffering from shell shock. We didn't know what to call it back then, but that's what was going on. I don't know what happened before I was born, but as a child, I only remember seeing him a few times.

As for my grandparents' occupations, I am not certain what Walter Sr. did other than the fact that he was a preacher. Where he preached, I'm not sure. Grandmother Willie G. did what we called at the time "day work." This was during deep segregation in the South. Work was very limited for Black people and most of the women did day work, which meant they worked in somebody's home, cleaning, cooking, taking care of kids, and those kind of things.

CHAPTER 6: THE HAWKINS PORTER SMITH FAMILY

Willie G. Hawkins *Claudia Hawkins*

I've never known and I'm not sure what my grandfather Walter did. I know that in Athens, Georgia where we are from, the Hawkins family were builders. They worked in construction and built houses. There was an entire neighborhood of Hawkins, and most of them had built their own home.

I have no idea about what grade school or middle school my grandparents may have gone to, but again, we're talking about the time of segregation. If you were Black during those days and lived in Memphis North Memphis, you went to Manassas. If you lived in South Memphis, you went to Booker T. Washington. All of the Hawkins family siblings attended Booker T. Washington High School.

My mother Ritta taught at Lester Elementary. So, I attended Lester. Well, let's go back further. Before that I went to Lutheran Cooperative. Our Aunt Claudia Hawkins taught there also. That would have been about 1953. I was five years old.

For elementary school I went to Manassas. My mother taught third grade at Manassas High School in North Memphis. It was high school grades one to twelve at the time, and I attended grades one through five at Manassas, as long as she taught there. That was outside of Lauderdale Sub in North Memphis.

The first couple of years we rode with a friend of hers and a sorority sister who lived nearby, and we rode to school with her. Then mother bought a car. My mother and my older brother Rob and I attended Manassas school.

After Manassas I went to Saint Anthony Catholic School from grades six through eight. That was also in North Memphis. First mother dropped us off. Later on, I rode the bus. It's very interesting, I rode the bus in my seventh-grade year because I've clarified this after talking to my brother (Roderick K. Porter Sr.).

When I started riding the bus in the seventh grade the buses were segregated, and in the middle of the school year, the buses were integrated. So, it was an interesting experience for a youngster. That would have been in about 1960.

For high school I went to Father Bertrand High School. That would have been 1962 to 1966. For college I went to Knox College in Galesburg, Illinois. I went there one year. I came back home and went to Memphis State University, where I graduated with a bachelor's degree. Then later on, I attended Memphis Theological Seminary. I got a master of divinity degree and then later I attended Eastern Baptist Seminary in Wynnewood, Pennsylvania, and that's where I got a doctorate of ministry degree.

My mother Ritta Hawkins and her sister Claudia Hawkins both graduated from LeMoyne-Owen College. I believe that some of the other sisters attended LeMoyne, but none of them graduated from LeMoyne. Mary graduated from District of Columbia Teacher's College in Washington, DC. She then went on to get her master's degree from George Washington University.

CHAPTER 6: THE HAWKINS PORTER SMITH FAMILY

My mother's first job was in Washington, DC. And after getting settled, she sent for Mary. My mother worked for the Treasury Department, and she sent for her sister Mary to also work in the government. Mary could type one hundred words per minute, so she was easily hired. Then later my mother sent for Aunt Sue. Uncle Walter went to the army, and he eventually moved to Washington, DC also. I am really not sure about Florence and Floretta and where they went to school.

I recall hearing Florence mention having gone to Fisk in Nashville and also to beauty school. She (Florence) also excelled in music. Floretta stayed close to home and took care of the family.

I know for sure that family church was Morning View Baptist Church, which is a stone's throw from the house on Carnegie. It seemed a long way as a child, but as an adult, it is literally a stone's throw away from the house. Most of the family at some point in time attended Morning View Baptist Church. My grandmother (Willie G. Hawkins) at some point in time joined Carnegie Church of God in Christ. Elder McNeal Sr. is the only paster I remember for Carnegie Church of God in Christ. I am not sure who was the pastor of Morning View when we were children.

So, when I was one year old my mother joined Metropolitan Baptist Church, and later Claudia joined Metropolitan Baptist Church. And from that point on Metropolitan was the church for us. Some of the rest of the family still attended Morning View, and of course, my grandma attended Carnegie Church of God in Christ until her death.

Grandma died in 1975 on October 31. 1658 Carnegie remained with our family until the 1990s. By then Claudia (who lived on Carnegie) moved in with mother (Ritta) who moved to McMillan Street when she remarried to Stanie Smith in late 1950s.

Ritta Porter Smith, teen Reginald Porter at 1671 McMillan St.

When the house at 1658 Carnegie Street was sold, it was bought by our neighbors the Givens family.

The house at 1671 McMillan remained in our family until somewhere around 2013. Ritta Hawkins Porter Smith passed in 2013, so we kept it until 2015 or 2016, something like that.

I grew up during the days of segregation, and so Black communities were separate. Schools were separate, everything was separate, but that created a sense of community. People grew up in the community, lived in the community, and as adults, they bought a house and continued to live there in the community.

Everybody knew everybody, went to school together and went to church together. It was supportive. Kids knew each other, the adults knew each other, the families knew each other, a lot of family married members of other families. So, the communities were very close-knit. Communities were kind of self-sufficient. There was the community store, the barber shop, and the beauty shop. Everything was right there in the community. And it was comfortable because wherever you went, you knew somebody.

CHAPTER 6: THE HAWKINS PORTER SMITH FAMILY

If you walked down the street, you knew most of the people and most people of the people knew who you were and who your family members were. And therefore, there was a degree of safety there and so communities were nurturing. You could, of course, sit on your porch at night. Whatever you needed was there in the community.

The atmosphere was always supportive. People knew when you were going off to college. If you played football on a team, everybody knew that you played football on that team, and if you did other things everybody knew about it. We shared things like Vacation Bible School. Kids went to Vacation Bible School at more than one church during summer. So, it was great atmosphere and a great place to grow up.

When thinking of the achievements of the people who came out of the neighborhood, I reflect on the fact that I spent most of my life in the ministry. I retired as pastor of Metropolitan Baptist Church, which was a significant thing because I am married to Rev. Davena Young Porter. As of June 2023, I have been married for fifty-three years.

Rev. Davena Young Porter & Dr. Reginald Porter Sr.

We have one son, Reginald Porter Jr. I have a daughter-in-law Sonya, and they are parents of twin daughters, which are my two granddaughters. These are things that I think are great accomplishments.

I'm very happy about a lot of the programs and lives that have been changed through the church. I have had the opportunity to speak at colleges and universities. I have taught about the Progressive National Baptist Convention, and I served as the regional vice president for the Southern Region of the Progressive Convention. I was president for a term of four years. We have tenure, so you can only be president for four years. I have taught at a seminary. I've taught both graduate school and undergraduate school. I've been a professional counselor. When the Church Health Center opened up, they only had a few employees. I was one of them. I was the counselor for the church's health centers for a couple of years.

As I celebrate what came out of the lineage of these people from the Lauderdale Sub, I'd have to mention my older brother Rod (Roderick) Porter. He was deputy director for the FCC (Federal Communications Commission) for at least thirty years, or more, maybe as many as forty years. My younger brother, Stan Smith, retired as a major in the Air Force. Of course, my mother and Aunt Claudia were both teachers. And I have a cousin who's been in movies and some people may know her as a TV star.

My mother's sister Sue became one of the first four Black lieutenants in the Washington, DC Police Department. That was Lieutenant Susie B. Hawkins in the early 1970s.

Also, my Uncle Walter G. Hawkins Jr. was a successful business owner in Washington, D.C. He got quite a reputation. He left Memphis and started working in media in Washington, DC. He worked with several television stations in the engineering department. At one point he owned his own gas station in DC.

CHAPTER 6: THE HAWKINS PORTER SMITH FAMILY

My Aunt Mary was a teacher as well. She was a supervisor of thirty-two schools in the District of Columbia's Special Education division. So, there were three teachers, my mother, my Aunt Claudia, and Aunt Mary.

My Aunt Florence (mother of LaRita Shelby) was an extremely accomplished pianist. Some of my fondest memories are of her, my cousins, and my aunts gathering around the piano at 1658 Carnegie Street while she played, and we sang.

Of course, while he didn't grow up in the Lauderdale Sub, my son (Dr. Reginald Porter Jr.) was deputy chief of staff for the Shelby County School System when the systems merged and created the second largest school system in the nation. He oversaw that merger. Reginald Jr. was also a senior vice president of Development and Corporate Social Responsibility at St. Jude's American Lebanese Syrian Associated Charities. Reginald Jr. later earned his doctorate in 2023 in Urban Higher Education.

Dr. Reginald Porter Sr. & Dr. Reginald Porter Jr.

When it comes to family values, well one of the most important things is that "family takes care of and provides for others." I know that my mother, and then later my Aunt Claudia (after they finished their education and got the jobs) provided for any of their siblings who wanted to go to school. They also were instrumental in helping to care for all of the children of the family, including making sure that they provided for any and all of them who may have wanted to attend school.

The family unit was important. My Aunt Floretta was the caretaker for my grandmother. My grandmother lost her legs at some point, and I remember that she (Floretta a.k.a. Buug) was the caretaker, and mother Aunt Claudia took care of her, so that she didn't have to want for anything. And so that system of care and provisions continued to the children and grandchildren all the way down the line.

It's important to take time to share memories like this because we need to know our history. Unfortunately, a lot of young people and the generations that are coming after us don't know and understand their history. They don't know what it meant to live in a segregated world, or in a segregated society, or to have opportunities intentionally withheld from them and then have to survive and achieve anyway. It's important to know that, and then it's important to understand where you have come from and how far you've come along.

When I was doing my doctoral work was when I really discovered the history after sitting down with my mother to talk about how our family get from Athens, Georgia, to Memphis. I learned how we lived with the Davenport family and all of the things that ensued from that and how the family evolved as a whole with the idea of loving and caring for one another.

My great Aunt Virginia invited our grandfather to come to Memphis. That's how it all started. So, the idea of caring for your family didn't just start with one generation. It was a carryover from that fact. I think that is very important for people to understand their present circumstance and appreciate it.

CHAPTER 6: THE HAWKINS PORTER SMITH FAMILY

Also in this family is Michael S. Washington (son of Floretta Hawkins) who was the director of Institutional Equity Title IX at the University of Memphis from 2015 to 2017. Prior to that he was the executive director of Human Resources Title IX at LeMoyne-Owen College. Michael's undergrad degree is from LeMoyne-Owen College in Memphis, and his master's degree is from Utah State.

Floretta's daughter Marqueline was an executive administrative assistant to the president of LeMoyne-Owen College for many years until her retirement in 2023. Floretta's other daughter Marcia Washington Seymour Austin holds a supervisor position at a major shipping company.

The sons of Mary Hawkins Johnson Haile (Sterling & Jackie Ray) were born in Washington, DC, where they both worked in law enforcement. Mary's grandsons Jackie Johnson Jr. works as a government contractor, Sterling Jr. earned a degree in economics and works for a major corporation, and Anthony Lamont Johnson is an internationally acclaimed bioscientist and Harvard Fellow.

Florence Hawkins' only daughter, LaRita Shelby, held nine titles in 1980, including Miss Black Memphis, Miss Black World of Tennessee, and Miss Black World. She won the Improved Benevolent Protective Order of Elks of the World (IBPOEW) National Oratorical Contest prior to that. She moved to Los Angeles to pursue the entertainment industry. From 1990 to 1997 she was an international radio personality for Armed Forces Radio where her self-titled show was heard in fifty-seven countries. Florence's grandson Justin is also pursuing music in Los Angeles.

Other grandchildren and great-grandchildren of this family in the Lauderdale Sub have earned degrees or exemplary career achievements in social work, customer service, culinary arts, and community service. David Allen Jr. (eldest son of Marqueline Gardner and first grandson of Floretta) has held many managerial positions, but he is most known and loved as Chef David in Memphis and surrounding areas. He is one of very few grandsons in the Hawkins family that had a real connection to the Lauderdale Sub and the houses that anchored his family foundations. All of Floretta Hawkins' grandchildren (David, Martin, Marcus, Ricky, Marissa, and Morgan) are working professionals.

Rod Porter Sr., Esq, Stanie Smith Ret Major USAF, Dr. Reginald Porter Sr.

My mother Ritta P.'s oldest son Roderick became the deputy chief of Mass Media for the FCC (Federal Communications Commission). He ended up writing satellite communication laws for the FCC's International Bureau.

Ritta's other grandchildren are Rod Jr. and, respectively, Stanie Smith Jr. (Ritta's youngest son) is a retired Air Force Major, and his son (Stanie II) has followed his father's legacy and served in the Air Force in Germany.

So, I've really learned that family not only takes care of each other, but their willingness to help care for other people extended beyond our blood relatives to other folks in the community.

CHAPTER 6: THE HAWKINS PORTER SMITH FAMILY

I suppose that that is where I learned a lot about the need and the value of taking care of your community and just the value of family in general. I learned the value of community and being a participant in the community, because my family was very much involved in the community and trying to make the community a better place.

CHAPTER 7

THE HODGES FAMILY

Memories of The Hodges Family from Fredericka Hodges

I am Fredericka Laverne Allen Hodges and I resided at 1501 Miller Street. My mother was Merle Allen. My father (Willie B. Allen) had a business in the back. We had two lots. So, he had a business where he sold wood and coal. People were using wood and coal, and he sold a lot of it on terms. He would keep a ledger of who would come to get wood and when they would come to pay.

CHAPTER 7: THE HODGES FAMILY

My father was very insightful in that he observed change and trends. I would say that more or less, he was a visionary. So, he saw where coal and wood would stop burning and that people had begun to start purchasing stoves. Electricity was coming in and they were no longer burning wood and coal. So, he started another business hauling cotton pickers and choppers. He really had several businesses. He would carry the people to Arkansas, which was Earle, Arkansas; Wynne, Arkansas and then he carried them to Walls, Mississippi.

The landowners paid my father $1.00 a head for transporting those day workers. So, he normally had 100. He had a bus and two trucks and that was his transportation business.

There were times when the cotton-picking business was no longer in season. You'd pick cotton in the fall. Then chopped it in the spring and summer. Well, in between that time, my father bussed children from Mississippi to the zoo.

So, he would go down and get the children who went to those little church schools, and he brought them to the zoo. Well, you could only do that on Thursdays and that was their outing. My father was from Senatobia, Mississippi and he knew several people who were schoolteachers and that's what he did.

He also saw that they (farmers) were using herbicides for keeping the grass out of the cotton. So, they had begun to use chemicals. Then the other part of it is that they had begun to use mechanical cotton pickers. My father saw that trend and he moved into contracting because a lot of building was going on.

He bought what I call the first robot. He bought a machine that loaded bricks. He bought a special truck with a machine that loaded bricks. He wanted to buy second truck and he did but it didn't have a machine on it. They didn't want to sell (to him) but they wanted to have a quota on the number of bricks that he could purchase from them. So, the truck would idle and that was a good sign of racism.

Also, where you saw African American males trying to get ahead, there was something in the system and the Jim Crow laws and all those other things. There's a new term that they use, I can't think of it right now. But it was the same thing that happened, where they are trying to change a policy where you can no longer do certain things.

He was a voter. He paid a poll tax and at that time the only people who could vote were people who owned property. So, my dad owned two houses in the Lauderdale Sub. He rented one out and we lived in the other one until the divorce.

After my parents divorced when I was thirteen, he moved into the other home. We had a lot of respect for money. We weren't wealthy or any of that, but we were taught to be frugal, not to waste, and not to tear up what you had because you'd have to buy it again. So, that was a very disciplined way to live.

My mother particularly, was very frugal. I can remember when we would buy a can of Ajax and we couldn't pull the whole peel back. She said pull back two holes and shake out whatever you needed to clean bathroom. She said that half the time you didn't do anything but shake it all out and half clean the tub. Which was true. So, we were very careful, very well disciplined, and careful with the way we utilized our resources.

There were five children in the household. My siblings were Sammie Steen, Willie, George, and Maurine. I was the oldest child and I used to do a lot by helping him. I learned that you cannot be afraid of change. I'm not afraid of change. When I see it, I try to see how I can benefit from it. There are a lot of changes getting ready to take place now with AI (artificial intelligence). What people have to do is read! You have to get exposed and then you have to see where you can fit into these changes.

CHAPTER 7: THE HODGES FAMILY

Here we are looking at people who are getting all bent out of shape over this AI and saying that is possibly going to destroy jobs. Well, if you think about it, you've already had some artificial intelligence exposure. That came with a voicemail. When you call an office, you don't get a receptionist anymore.

You may get voicemail that directs you to the various areas of the business. So, that's a form of artificial intelligence. It's not anything that's totally new. The same thing occurred when the internet came in. People used to call the airline to make a reservation. You became the reservationist. It's going to be a lot of change with technology and people have to prepare for those changes and also prepare their children.

One of the best things that could happen today is to be aware of children who have good mathematic skills. They will be at the top of the ladder, because they will have opportunities. That means that you have to make sure your child is getting a good education so that they can compete. There is no reason to be afraid. We understood change and prepared for it.

My family lived in the Lauderdale subdivision from 1938 to I would say 1993 or 1994, maybe longer than that. We lived in the same community. That's where my mother lived, but, after you go to school and then marry, you don't live there. However, the family home was still there into the late 1990's in to the year 2000.

Our first neighbors were White. Between 1938 (my birth year) and 1952 that was an integrated neighborhood. So, my neighbors were White. For thirteen years we had White neighbors. My next-door neighbor was White. Her name was Mrs. Pearl Doris. She had a son. He didn't live with her. His name was Bobby Doris. Up the street we had a contractor that lived next door to her. His name was Mr. Kitts. He had one son. I remember his name was EJ Kitts. So that community started changing from about 1954 to 1956. That White flight went to Long View Heights. South Side School was over there in the area where South Side Park is.

The names of my family members are Sammie Steen Allen Bradford, Willie Merle Allen Franklin, George Robert Allen is my brother, and a younger sister Maurine Delores Allen. Maurine happened to have married a member of the Allen family, but of course she's divorced. Maurine Delores Allen. Those are my siblings.

I attended Lincoln Elementary School and Hamilton High School. I finished grade school in 1952 and I finished high school in 1956. After that I attended Tennessee State University on a Kroger scholarship. Then, I took a job working in the library there in the reference department. We had a family friend, and her name was Sadie Gassaway. Her sister taught at Booker T. Washington. She was a math teacher at Tennessee State. She was instrumental in my getting that job. I worked in that particular library for four years.

Kortrecht graduating class of 1871, according to BlackThen.com

CHAPTER 7: THE HODGES FAMILY

I practically worked my way through college with the scholarship money. I received two additional scholarships. I was awarded the Delta Sigma Theta scholarship and then I was also awarded the G. P. Hamilton scholarship because I had the highest grade point average in my freshman year of any student from Memphis. So, that scholarship money really helped.

> **Note:** *G. P. Hamilton is the author of The Bright Side of Memphis. He was principal of Kortrecht School (formerly named Clay Street School). It was the first public high school for Blacks in Memphis in 1873. Its name was changed in 1891. In 1911 Kortrecht was the only Black public high school in the city. In 1926 Kortrecht High School relocated to a new building and became Booker T. Washington High School. community rich in history and tradition. Source: Kortrecht High School, Miscellaneous Photos and Articles (memphistechhigh.com)*

After I married, I went back to school, and I went to Ole Miss, The University of Mississippi. That's when I got my master's degree. My last teaching position was at Shelby State College at that time, which is now known as Southwest College.

The sense of unity in the community in the Lauderdale Sub was simply this. We had a village. Everyone was involved in protecting the children in the community, disciplining the children and the church was one of the cornerstones of the community. The schools were another cornerstone, as were the individual families.

We didn't have the opportunity to venture too far because there were so many limitations. The term I was trying to think I was autocracy. Jim Crow is a form of autocracy, so when you hear the term autocracy, it is nothing new. It just has some new ways of looking at things.

There are limitations and policies. These policies set limitations. We didn't have a swimming pool in the community, but we could go to certain areas in the community where we could swim. You could go to

Lincoln Park, which was in our area. There was a pool in Orange Mound, and there was a pool in North Memphis.

Basically, the community was so supportive of each other, that if somebody needed a cup of flour, you'd go next door. Then, when you got the flour, you brought that cup back. That's the kind of community that we had.

The neighbors knew one another. It was different. It was all about taking care of each other. We realized where we were in the system. It was segregated, but it was protected.

As for the people in my family, no adult drank (liquor) in front of children. Now we could smell it on them, but actually seeing them drink it was a "no- no." Now, of course, we couldn't use profanity in our house. Even though we had cousins who would say things, we wanted to repeat what they said but we couldn't.

So, we had to say: "So and so talking bad talk." The profanity that I heard was when I went to college. I didn't know that folks could cuss like that, but they can. It was just some things that some families didn't do. That's it. There were some rules about that.

So many high achievers came out of this area. I think that it was a value system. I think that people who didn't have opportunities to go further wanted their children to do so. They made sacrifices for that to occur. That was one of the reasons you wanted to see your children go as far as they could go.

You didn't set limits. You had to have expectations, high expectations. That's what happened in the neighborhood. People who couldn't read would say; "Get all you can, because once you get something in your head, nothing can take that away from you."

Which was true. It's still true. I can remember, I wrote letters for my godmother. I didn't know she couldn't write. I wrote letters to her family, and she would tell me what to say. I wrote the letters, and we mailed it. Then, believe it or not, they wrote her letters back, I would read them to her. Apparently, she couldn't read. I didn't know that. I didn't think about it, but there were a lot of people who couldn't read. But they were encouraging children to work hard and stay in school.

Another thing we have to always remember, is that we are minorities. We are African American people. So, your opportunities for going up that ladder are going to be more difficult. You're not going to get a good push from anybody, except for a few family members. So, you have to be as prepared as you can and have confidence that you will have to work harder to stay in whatever position you obtain. That will not change. When you start thinking people want an easy road, everybody is on it. You have to develop your competences and stay on top of your game because if you don't, they'll take it away from you.

CHAPTER 8

THE MOORE FAMILY

*Memories of The Moore Family from
Carrie Moore Black*

Carrie Mae Moore Black

CHAPTER 8: THE MOORE FAMILY

I am Carrie Mae Moore Black. For starters, let me add something right here. On my parents' property deed, it says the Orleans Subdivision. That Lauderdale Sub was a title given to that area and it has lived on.

Actually, it was the Orleans Subdivision better known as the Lauderdale Sub. Lauderdale Street happens to be the main drag between Parkway and Person where Black folks resided.

I have no idea when it became known as that. I know that information for a fact from my parents' deed. Perhaps everybody wasn't a homeowner, but my parents were.

I was born at 1673 Carnage Street. Somewhere between the age of six and six and a half, my parents purchased a home at 1674 McMillan Street. It was one street over from where I was born. I was actually born at home. My father was Humphrey Taft Moore Sr. My mother was Bessie Collins. Collins was her maiden name.

Let's go back a little bit first. My father was also known as Umphrey. It's interesting to me that just in some little chatter among family, my grandmother never called my father or pronounced his name as Humphrey. She always said Umphry. (She did not pronounce the "H.") Okay, so is my understanding that folk whose name was Umphrey began to be called Humphrey, with the emergence and popularity of Humphrey Bogart.

He was also known as Jake. I am sharing pronunciation but listening to my grandmother, she said "Umphrey" and he was named after her brother.

My dad was born long before the evolution of Humphrey Bogart but the pronunciation of his name became Humphrey with the emergence of the actor Humphrey Bogart.

There were seven children in our family. I am the seventh child. The oldest is Martha Jane Moore Waterford. Next is Rosie Moore Gibbs.

Then there is Bernice Moore Hoyle. Next is Humphrey Taft Moore Jr. Then there is Peter Moore, Ola Nell Moore Williams, and Carrie Mae Moore Black.

I grew up in a loving two parent home with the five girls, me being the fifth, and two boys. My memories include, of course, the things that we did together. There was not a lot of first outside socialization apart from the church, you see. My childhood was happy and my home was my safe place.

As the youngest child, I was more than a little spoiled and pampered and the center of attention. There were a lot of influences in my development, both in the home and outside of the home.

I grew up in a community that shared. Some of the most favorable memories are sharing daily meals at the table that began with the blessing offered by the parents and followed by a Bible verse from each individual child at the table.

Among those siblings, he didn't grow up as a sibling to me, of course, because he was much older, but my parents also raised my mother's youngest brother, David James Collins, who grew up with the older children.

My parents had five children when they moved to Memphis. Two children were born in Memphis, and that was me and my sister Ola Nell. We called her Nell. The difference between Nell's age and the fifth child that they brought with them from Mississippi was eight years. So, there you have a picture of what the family group looked like.

As I told you, my family were homeowners, and we lived on a corner lot, which gave us access to everyone in our neighborhood from all walks of life. They traveled on foot or in the few vehicles that were going and coming from work, bus stops, grocery stores, churches and visiting neighbors. Because during the time period that you gave me in the 40s

CHAPTER 8: THE MOORE FAMILY

to 60s, there was a lot of walking. There was a lot of bus riding. There was friendliness in the neighborhood and people stopped and chatted and that kind of thing.

My family's religious belief, of course, was Christianity. It was practiced in the traditional African American Baptist Church. Our congregation was the largest in the neighborhood. There were three Baptist churches, one Methodist Church and one Pentecostal church that was in the immediate neighborhood.

We had an interesting community because Caucasians always lived all around us situated in sort of what I always think of as a horseshoe. But there was little to no social interaction between the groups. We shared the same grocery stores, drugstores, variety stores and family practice doctors that were all within walking distance. But everyone in my school and my church looked just like me. The Family Church was Morning View Missionary Baptist Church was at 1623 Carnegie Street.

The children attended Lincoln Elementary from first to eighth grade. At an eighth grade graduation, we have pictures of every child in the family and their eighth grade graduation group.

And then from there, we went to Booker T. Washington. That was your school of choice, the older children relished the idea of going to Booker T. Washington. There were only three schools that were notable as I remember in the Memphis area for African Americans, and that was Booker T. Washington, Manassas, and Hamilton School. There was Melrose out in Orange Mound. It was not as much mentioned and was not the school that the children from this area would go to.

Our family values centered on faith in God, honesty, education, and a good work ethic. My parents provided for us. My father was a truck driver. My earliest memory of my mother is that she was a seamstress. Later my mother worked as the head cook at Lincoln Elementary School and then after that she worked at Sea Isle School. She retired from that job as the chief union steward. My father retired as a truck driver from M. E. Carter and Company.

I grew up with the pride of knowing that my dad was known as an excellent provider. So that was a great source of pride in that era for a man to have such notable reputation because my parents provided for us in such a manner that people outside of our immediate experience, were often surprised to learn that we were a family of seven children.

My church family, the neighborhood school and my home were a close-knit band during that time. It gave meaning to what is now the cliché. "It takes a village." That is in fact the way the community that I grew up in operated. You see our neighborhood was composed of all walks of life.

At the time we hadn't been separated into economic groups. That emerged in the late 1950's and early 1960's and that kind of thing. In our neighborhood there might have been our preachers and pastors and our teachers. We were all a neighborhood family.

And when I say that it took a village, now in 2023, everywhere you go, you're under the watchful eye of cameras everywhere. Well, if you will, there were cameras then because as children walked from school to church to the playground or to visit a neighbor's house, somebody's eyes were always on the children.

There were those who would offer correction if they saw the child step out of line with no reprisal. So, children walked in such a way for the most part, that any report that went to their family's house would be a good one. Because if a child stepped out of line, the person had no problem with either taking a walk to the child's house, walking the child back home, or picking up the telephone to report behavior that was not expected from that child from a certain family. So, we were on our P's and Q's all the time. We had noteworthy mentors and role models all around our neighborhood.

CHAPTER 8: THE MOORE FAMILY

Another fond memory is the fact that my grandmother was just within walking distance. She was less than two blocks away from me growing up and also, let me throw this in. She was my first Sunday School teacher. She was articulate, bright, and well spoken. She taught Sunday school until she became very old. She died at 97, lucid and with all intentions of coming back to church to teach.

Grandmother's name was Martha Jane Edwards. My oldest sister Martha Jane is named after her. First, she lived at 1573 Carnegie Street and when she died, I believe that she was living at 1723 McMillan. When I was growing up that was not a part of the African American section of McMillan Street. The racial divide stopped at Person Street until the early 1960s and then it expanded. The parameters of the so-called Lauderdale Sub were Person Street and when she moved, she was on the other end of McMillan. So, she lived on Carnegie, then McMillan, and so did I.

Work ethics were very important. The children emerged from a family of people, starting with the older people, who were not formally educated. There emerged from this family, college degrees, engineers and there were family members in management. My brother Peter was the first to go to college from this family. He went to Tennessee Statue A and I (college of agriculture and industry) in 1956 or 1957. He graduated from the College of Engineering in 1960 and he was the first.

None of the girls had a college degree except me. I have a bachelor of science degree in psychology and a master of divinity degree. My sister Nell has a certificate of graduation from the now defunct Henderson Business College. It was a secretarial school and ended her career first as bookkeeper, secretary and she bookkeeper and she retired as a teller at a bank.

At that time the encouragement for education was extended to the other generations. And now we have to add to that PhD's, at least three master's degrees, and a few bachelor's degrees as the generations continued.

My granddaughter Raven Carrie has a master's degree. She got both of her degrees at the University of Tennessee at Knoxville from the School of Information and Communication.

She went abroad between her bachelor's degree and her master's degree. She did a stint of intense study at the University of Dublin, Ireland. I also have a niece who has earned a PhD. That's the highest level that has been attained from coming down these generations.

Following the legacy of faith in our community, I am a member of the clergy having been ordained in 1995 and I'm now Pastor of Second Congregational United Church of Christ here in Memphis. I learned to read at the age of four, and among the first reading materials that I was exposed to was the Bible and Bible storybooks, My Little Golden Books, the newspaper *Commercial Appeal,* and those little reading cards for beginners that I had in my grandmother's Sunday school class.

These early experiences shaped my imagination and my belief in God, and I can't remember a time in my early childhood when I didn't want to be baptized. I was granted that privilege at the age of nine.

I remember the Westbrooks family. I remember Pearl especially. Pearl had this outstanding outgoing personality. And I remember that their father did something for the *Memphis World* or the *Tri-State Defender* newspapers, but I believe it was the *Memphis World*.

There was a Westbrooks family member who was almost paired with each Moore. Gloria was my age. Pearl is on the eighth grade graduation photo with one of my brothers. Shirley is on the eighth grade graduation photo with one of my sisters. Logan is on the eighth grade graduation photo with one of my sisters and then the Westbrook family moved away

CHAPTER 8: THE MOORE FAMILY

from Carnegie Street. We were on the same street so, I always knew the Westbrooks.

There was also never a time when I didn't know the Hawkins because they too lived on Carnegie Street. Two of the Hawkins sisters (Ritta Hawkins Porter Smith and Claudia Hawkins) were among those role models that I spoke of.

Ritta and Claudia were among those schoolteachers who were in our neighborhood. As close as our neighborhood was, not everybody really knew them. But personally, I can tell you that they were role models for me.

Even as I grew and Ritta married the widower across the street (Stanie Robin Smith Sr.) from me (on McMillan). We then became even closer. As I grew into mature adulthood, and at the time of her death, I was addressing her as Ritta P. That's how it was. We had become good friends as mature adults. Claudine had become very, very fond of my parents and us.

I used to like walking from my house to Morning View church or walk to the malt stand as a little girl, because as I said, I was invited to speak when Claudia died and I mentioned how it just built my ego for Mrs. Smith and Miss Claudia to say, "Oh, she's so cute. Oh, she's so smart." That was loaded for me to have a compliment like that coming from them.

I am happy to add that I can remember street by street those influences that were not only a part of my life, but I believe with Logan (Westbrooks) being far ahead of me in age, it was a part of their lives too. With the residents of that area, there was such pride in that neighborhood. As I said, everybody did not own a home, but I do remember that for some years in my whole block, there was nothing but homeowners. So that also was a source of pride.

We had so many people in the neighborhood who influenced not only me and my sister who came later, but those who were before us from the oldest sister down to and Logan. He was the age of my second oldest, but he knew all the rest of them, because he was in contact with my brother whenever he came to town.

I always heard about Logan and how brilliant he was. It was as if I knew him myself because during that time, we took pride in those who had moved away. You know, technology is wonderful. It's absolutely wonderful but nothing will take the place of those evenings sitting on the porch in chair and having ice cream or watching TV eating popcorn in the backyard and sharing memories of those people who used to live in the neighborhood.

And as a young woman, having heard stories over and over, they became personal to me as if I knew these people for myself and took a walk with them. But there were so many older people who influenced from the oldest to the youngest in these families that you are looking at, you see. I remember them with fondness because they spent their lives in this little neighborhood, and they spent their lives loving and caring about the generations that came after them. My grandmother was known as Mother Edwards because she was a mother in Morning View Baptist Church. She was very well respected for her teaching and her demeanor.

CHAPTER 9

THE NEELY FAMILY

Memories of The Neely Family from James Neely

James Neely

My family lived in the Lauderdale Subdivision during the time frame of the 1940s–1970s, which is the era that this book is focused upon. My father had a trucking business and we lived on Lauderdale Street and Logan Westbrooks lived one street over. I was always associated with Logan from grammar school to high school and growing up we were always competitors.

We would build go-karts. We'd always try to see who could build the fastest go kart. We also traded comic books. I would go over to his house, and we'd swap comic books. His daddy was a promoter for *the Memphis World* newspaper and a lot of kids in the neighborhood would go out with Mr. Westbrooks and sell the papers all over the city, primarily in the Black neighborhoods.

Alphonso Westbrooks Sr. and the Memphis World newsboys

I was always associated with Logan growing up as well as his family and his sisters. Back in those days, that's when neighborhoods were like a community where you knew each other. You knew the mothers, you knew the fathers, the sisters, and brothers. We just shared everything during that time. It was a great time.

After high school I went into the Air Force and Logan went on to college. And from there, his life just took off in the record business. He was sent over to Africa and other places, and he was always just a unique person. Even in high school, when we had programs in the auditorium, Logan was always the one on stage talking. He's quite a spokesperson with great knowledge. I was telling him recently, it's amazing how we all came from a poor family but there's a difference from being a poor person than a "Po" person. So, we were poor, but we weren't "Po."

We all helped each other. I was telling him that it's amazing how we came from such diverse places. We grew up from that time with expectations that we could do anything. When you grew up in a world where we as Black people were indoctrinated in the idea that we were N*ggers. At that rate you got to really be strong and have good foresight to be able to see things and imagine: "Yes, I can do this. Nothing can stop me." That's the way it was when I came out of the Air Force.

I came back to Memphis for a year and after just one year, I said: "No. I can't stay here." This had to be 1958 or 1959. "I can't be nobody's 'Boy' no more. I can't say 'Yes sir and No sir' to you, and you abuse me." So, I left, and I went to California and I swore to God that I would never come back looking for a job. The only way that I would come back to Memphis was if I bought a job with me. And that's how I ended up coming back to Memphis in the 1970s.

In California I was in the insurance business at United Insurance Company of America. I had made a lot of contacts and being with a major company, I acquired a lot of knowledge on insurance. Every time I would come back to Memphis, I would always see people still buying burial insurance. Here it is 1974 and Black people were still paying 25 cents a week here. 25 cents on one child and 25 cents on another child. I knew I could take all those quarters and put it together and make it $70 or $80 a month and then I can give the father $15,000 or better in whole life insurance and cover the wife and the children too. And I said, "There's a market here." I came back and that was my goal to tap that market. From there things just went and that's pretty much the story on me and Logan.

We still communicate and keep in contact. At one time, I had a top politician (he's dead now) named Roscoe Dixon who came to my office and asked me: "Man, what is it that you're doing?" I had tapped the market selling insurance to government employees and I had endorsements from the unions. I learned how to do that from a lot of Jewish guys that I was working with in California. I covered Tennessee and Louisiana. I did great down in New Orleans, Nashville, and Memphis. I had an office in all of those locations, and this was with a Booker T. Washington High School education. You know when I was doing millions in the barbecue business, there wasn't a "stop him" thought nowhere in my dream.

The Neely family lived at 1559 South Lauderdale. My father became fairly wealthy back in the 1930s. It really started in the late 1920s. And we were one of the first houses on Lauderdale South of Parkway. My dad built a four-bedroom brick home, with indoor plumbing bathrooms. We were one of the few homes that had indoor toilets on Lauderdale during that time.

Oust LeMoyne Sit-In Students From Part-Time Jobs

Plunkett   Miss Edwards   Miss Robertson

In Memphis, three LeMoyne college students who participated in sit-ins at Memphis public libraries were fired from their part-time jobs. Coeds Jevita Edwards and Kate Jean Robertson were both discharged from positions at St. Joseph Hospital, a Catholic institution, and Marvin Plunkett, 21, who had been employed at the American Legion Club for about eight years, was notified by an official that he was "laid off indefinitely." An administrator at the hospital said the LeMoyne coeds were discharged because they did not report to work and did not call to say they would be in. Both coeds were arrested and jailed for trying to obtain books which were not available at a small Negro branch library.

CHAPTER 9: THE NEELY FAMILY

I had a friend of mine who grew up on Lauderdale also. His name was Garnett Brown. He had a sister named Margaret, a sister named Jean and a baby brother that was named Samuel Brown. Garnett became a noted musician. His sister Jean Francois Brown was one of the seven or eight that marched and became known as the LeMoyne Seven or the LeMoyne Eight, or something like that. Jean was one of those. Allen Stiles was also a part of the LeMoyne sit-ins.

> **Note:** *The aforementioned is in reference to the 1960 Memphis Sit-In Movement. On March 18, 1960, seven students initiated a sit-in at the McClellan's Variety Store lunch counter on downtown Memphis. The students were from Owen Junior College. Student organized sit-ins were taking place all over the country. On March 19, 1960, thirty-six students from LeMoyne-Owen College and Owen Junior College participated in a sit-in at the Cossitt and Peabody public libraries. The students were arrested, along with five African American journalists. The event is known as the 1960 Memphis Sit-In Movement, led by LeMoyne graduate Marion Barry, national chairman of the Student Non-Violent Coordinating Committee (SNCC). (Source: HMdb.org)*

Garnett Brown Photo: Legacy.com

Garnett became a noted musician living in New York. I caught him once on TV with Sammy Davis Jr. in Acapulco, Mexico. He got married and had two daughters. With the music industry the way that it was, in order to be more stable, he moved to Los Angeles. He went to Arkansas State at Pine Bluff. That's where he graduated. He then went to LA, and he became a schoolteacher. He taught English but he still did music work. He did musical arrangements, and he was a producer. He also did the musical arrangement for the movie Harlem Nights.

A woman named Johnnie Turner was the Tennessee State Representative for District 85. She gave tours of Memphis, and she recognized Garnett. They had this thing where they gave you a plaque. It was at the New Daisy Theater about ten or twelve years ago.

When Garnett came to Memphis, he always stayed with me at my home. I'm the one that introduced him and brought him on stage. He had to take a leave of absence to go out and perform with different bands. He passed away October 9, 2021 but I keep in touch with his sister Margaret. She lives in Little Rock. In fact.

My mom was a stay-at-home mom. In my early life growing up, I remember every morning when we woke up we had hot biscuits. We had a complete breakfast every morning. In later years, I think by the time I got into maybe the eighth or ninth grade, my mom became a nurse. They called it a vocational nurse and she spent her time working at John Gaston Hospital and different hospitals until they all moved out to California in early 1958.

We never sold our home. My sister is the only one still living in Memphis. They never lived anywhere but Memphis. My sister was in college and then she became a teacher here in Memphis. Her name is Shirley Neely. My mother became a nurse and I guess after I came out of the military, my attitude was so different. I wasn't a boy anymore. If you looked at me like you're gonna say something wrong to me, then I was on you like grits on Al Green baby. Look here. C'mon, "That ain't gonna fly."

I went to Lincoln Elementary on Orleans Street, along with Gilbert Earl Patterson. He was behind me in years, but his sister Barbara was in our class. I also knew the Koens very well. There was a Koen family that had a laundry on the corner of Essex and Orleans.

Garnett Brown had a cousin named George Koen. He was a bright, light person and he loved to sing. The Koen family was big in Lauderdale Sub.

George Koen, son of Robert Koen with Bertha Koen

Koen's Cleaners Photo: Courtesy of Delia Koen

Margaret Alice Koen, George Koen, son of Robert Koen, and Ollie Davis. Photo: Courtesy of Delia Koen

CHAPTER 9: THE NEELY FAMILY

Miss Koen was a grown lady probably in her thirties when I was a kid aged ten or eleven years old. She'd have to be about 125 or 130 years old if she were still living. She was a big light skinned woman. She lived over on Beale Street, 330 Beale Street, or something like that. They had a shoe repair shop on Beale and 4th Street.

My daddy's barber was named Mr. Bibb. He lived upstairs in that building on Beale Street above Dr. Vincent's dental office. My dad would go to the barbershop. In the summertime nobody had air conditioning. There weren't any fire escapes. If you sat in the windows, you'd be looking down on Beale Street. If you get off balance, you're going down. I'd sit up there and look down on Beale Street while visiting Dr. Vincent's office.

I attended Olivet Baptist Church, with the great Rev. Lonzie Odie (L. O.) Taylor, who was pastor from 1931 to 1956. As for college, I attended Metro Bible College in Los Angeles.

In the 1940s we were a family of nine children. My dad had trucks and we would be spic and span. On Sunday morning my dad would get up, put concrete blocks on either side and he'd lay a plank over them to make a bench and we'd sit on that plank and ride down to Olivet Baptist Church. It wasn't until 1950 when my parents bought their first car. It was a 1950 black Pontiac.

We used to go everywhere on the back of that truck. My dad had relatives over in Forrest City, Arkansas. Some Sundays after church, he'd make some sideboards. We're talking about trucks that were about twenty feet long. He'd put some side boards on so that we'd be safe when we went to Arkansas.

I have a big family down in Mississippi. My mother had a brother down there and the only time I ever remember seeing him was when he would catch the bus from down there in Mississippi. It's about fifty or sixty miles to go from down there.

He was a World War II veteran. He would come up and go to the VA hospital for doctor visits. We would see stay with him at the bus station him it was time for him to get back on the bus. Now can you imagine this? This is probably 1946, 1947, or 1949.

I had relatives living sixty miles away in Mississippi and I had five or six cousins that I never met until I was fully grown. Sixty miles at that time was like going to Chicago or California. You ain't got no reliable transportation. You know? It's just the way it was.

I left South Lauderdale on January 3, 1955. I was out of school for a twelfth-grade Christmas break. Instead of going back, I joined the Air Force. Also, on December 30,. four days prior to that, I became a first-time father. I was seventeen years old and two months. My daughter Stephanie Joy Neely was born. You'll find her at the restaurant every day.

One of my most beloved photos is a family picture in our front room sitting on my sofa with all nine of us, including our mom and dad at our home in the Lauderdale Sub.

CHAPTER 9: THE NEELY FAMILY

Note: *In 1978 James Neely opened Jim Neely's Interstate Bar-B-Que on South Third Street in Memphis. It would be the first in a chain of nationally acclaimed restaurants throughout the city. James returned to California in 1985 to purchase a bar-b-que joint named Jay Bee's in Compton. It had originally inspired him and it's open today, still serving Memphis style bar-b-que. Another location JR's Barbeque is operated by his sister Beverly in Culver City, California.*

JR's Barbeque in Culver City, California

The Neely name is now synonymous with great Memphis flavored bar-b-que. James' nephews and other family members have continued his legacy in the food industry.

Memories of The Neely Family from Shirley Neely

Shirley Claire Neely

I am Shirley Claire Neely. My family, the Neely family, included my mother, my father and my grandmother who lived with us. We lived at 1559 South Lauderdale. My father owned a hauling contract business, which he contracted exclusively with Fischer Lime and Cement Company.

We lived at 1559 South Lauderdale. My father moved to that address in 1927 and he lived there until 1958 when he and his wife moved to Los Angeles, California. My siblings are Faye Catherine, Delores Ann,

CHAPTER 9: THE NEELY FAMILY

William Jr., James Neely, Gloria Neely, Shirley Neely, Harry, Beverly, and Patricia Neely.

My mother attended Booker T. Washington. My siblings in the elementary level went to Lincoln Elementary and Saint Augustine Elementary. All but two of my siblings are graduates of Booker T. Washington High School.

My father was a hauling contractor for the Fischer Lime and Cement Company. He started working there about 1919 and he stayed there until 1958.

My mother, Jessie Neely, was a stay-at-home mother until all of her children entered school and she went back to school and became a nurse.

At our early age we attended Olivet Baptist Church on Calhoun Street and later we attended Saint Augustine Catholic Church. Faye Neely Hudson attended LeMoyne-Owen College, and I think she graduated in 1953. Then she also graduated from University of Michigan at Ann Arbor, and that was in the 1960s. She received a degree in Social Work from LeMoyne and the master's degree from the University of Michigan was also in Social Work. She was a social worker.

As for me, upon graduating from LeMoyne-Owen College, I became an elementary school principal. I also attended the University of Memphis in 1972 and received a master's degree in elementary education, special education K–12 and I received certification in elementary administration.

I graduated with my first master's degree in 1972 and I continued until 1981. I became a teacher, and I worked as a fifth grade teacher, and a special ed teacher. Then I became an elementary school assistant principal, and later I was a principal at Gordon Elementary. For the last four years of my job, I was on loan from the Memphis City Schools to the Tennessee Department of Education, where I became an evaluator of a program initiated by Governor Lamar Alexander. My father owned a 1925 Packer and a number of trucks that he used in this business. He owned maybe five or six trucks.

My family was very close and we did a lot of things together. We went on trips to visit special attractions and attended as many activities as we could at that time. Blacks were only able to attend the zoo of the Mid South Fair on special days, but we all went to them. We used to have a habit in the summertime of going to Airways Blvd and we would park our cars. We'd take picnic baskets and watch the airplanes land and take off. We also always had special activities that we did within our church and our school.

I was the last person to live on Lauderdale and I was there from 1940 to 1972. It was my mother's home and at that particular time I wanted my own house. So, I moved.

Note: *Shirley Neely is the author of The History of The Neely Family: Many Homelands, One Family © 2009. Published by*

Shirley C. Neely: Memphis, TN 2021.

CHAPTER 10

THE PATTERSON FAMILY

*Memories of the Patterson family from
Cheryl Hall, niece of Bishop G. E. Patterson*

Bishop G. E. Patterson

I am Cheryl "Cherie" Hall, a descendant of Bishop W. A. Patterson Sr. and Mary Patterson, who at one time lived in the Lauderdale subdivision. They were my maternal grandparents.

Mary Patterson (August 3, 1901–May 30, 1981) was the wife of Bishop W. A. Patterson Sr. They produced W. A. Patterson Jr., Gilbert Earl (G. E.), Mary (Hawkins), Barbara (Davis) and the middle daughter, Lee Ella Patterson Smith. W. A. Jr. was the pastor of New Jerusalem Church of God in Christ (COGIC) in Detroit until his death in 1988.

Bishop William Archie Patterson Sr. (April 30, 1898–Nov. 4, 1991) Brother of Bishop J. O. Patterson Sr. and father of COGIC Bishop G.E. Patterson

CHAPTER 10: THE PATTERSON FAMILY

Bishop J.O. Patterson Sr.

Bishop J.O. Patterson Jr. son of J.O. Patterson Sr. and Deborah Indiana Mason. He is the grandson of Bishop Charles Mason, cofounder of the Church of God in Christ.

My parents are Lee Ella Patterson Smith and Bishop Samuel Smith. I have a sister named Barbara Joyce Boatner. W. A. Patterson Sr. was the brother of J. O. Patterson Sr.

James Oglethorpe Patterson Sr. (popularly known as J. O. Patterson Sr.) was the father of J. O. Patterson Jr., who was the cousin of Gilbert Earl (G. E.) Patterson. J.O. Patterson Sr. and G.E. Patterson both became Presiding Bishops of the Church of God in Christ. Bishop J. O. Patterson, Sr. was married to Deborah Mason, who was Bishop Charles Mason's daughter. So, there's definitely a family legacy in the Church of God in Christ (COGIC).

The Pattersons were very involved in the Church of God in Christ. They served faithfully. Bishop C. H. Mason was the founder of our church that was chartered in 1907 and in 1915 he won the legal rights to the name. He was influenced by his experience in 1907 when he visited the Azusa Street Revival in Los Angeles, California. It is said that this is where he was baptized in the Holy Spirit and began to speak in tongues.

My father Samuel Smith married my mom in 1952, and I have heard a few times what Big Momma Mary Patterson told my mom about my dad when he accepted the ministry.

She said, "You know, he was already bootlegging ministering in his own way, but then he officially accepted the call." My mom said she never wanted to be a preacher's wife, but that's kind of what happens to PK's (preacher's kids). That's how they came into the ministry together.

They founded the South Side Church of God in Christ. My dad served faithfully to both Bishop Mason and to the church that he founded. Bishop Mason used to call my dad his "long, tall boy" because my dad was six foot four. He would drive Bishop Mason around and then he served faithfully in the Tennessee headquarters. This was Bishop J. O. Patterson's jurisdiction until he went to the Tennessee Fourth. That's where Bishop G. E. Patterson became a jurisdictional bishop.

CHAPTER 10: THE PATTERSON FAMILY

My dad and my mom created the wording for the original Young People Willing Workers (YPWW). The YPWW is the International Youth Department of the Church of God in Christ (COGIC). My dad also formed the Clergy Bureau of Identification and that was acknowledged by Bishop G. E. There's a very long integrated history with COGIC. I'm proud to say I'm COGIC, but I'm also proud when I know that people represent the unadulterated gospel, the Father, Son, and the Holy Ghost.

My father, Bishop Samuel Smith was the administrative assistant to Bishop G. E. Patterson, until he became the presiding bishop. A lot of people assumed that my father would roll into that role, but my father stood up in a meeting when all the bishops were there from the General Board. He asked if he could make a statement. He said that we have someone here who is younger and who is more equipped for the job. He said: "If you have no objection, I'd like to nominate Jerry Maynard to be appointed the Jurisdictional Bishop of the Tennessee Fourth." Everyone agreed with the appointment.

The role was 100% unanimous. The bishops were amazed. They said they had never seen anyone who was so selfless as to nominate someone to an office that could have easily held themselves. All of the bishops agreed.

That's how Bishop Jerry L. Maynard Sr. became the jurisdictional bishop for the Tennessee Fourth.

Southside Church definitely has a legacy in the city as well. We used to have evangelistic services on Saturday nights. They worked with Teen Challenge and may have even worked with the Billy Graham crusade a couple times. They were very involved in South Memphis. The church is located on McLemore.

I was touched by what happened within my lifetime. Bishop J. O. Patterson, Sr. was already the presiding bishop when I came along and to me, they were my uncles and my grandfather. It wasn't until my mid-teens and early twenties, when I was around other people that I realized the enormity of my lineage and what a legacy it is. I had very down-to-earth parents as well as my other family. Bishop G. E. Patterson was also very down-to-earth, considering his position. To me, they were just my family.

I also remember that my uncles were avid fishermen. They really enjoyed that. As far as the work ethic, my uncle was very organized. He also introduced the tithe of tithes. This meant that instead of imposing all these different assessments and payments for the jurisdiction, he suggested a tithe of tithes. This means just take 10% of the tithes that are collected and use those funds to help take care of church business. I think there were still some other assessments, but he didn't want to gouge the people. He made sure that the jurisdiction operated at an increase, not a deficit. He desired that whatever needed to be taken care of could be taken care of from the coffers. So, those are the things I remember hearing about as far as how he ran business. As far as I knew, the church didn't have a mortgage when he was there. They were pretty much debt free from that regard. He just knew how to properly orchestrate things and not and not be reliant on chicken dinners to defray the cost of running the ministry.

He created a radio station. He created the school that he had for a moment and all that he did was for the betterment of other people, from what I understand. I'm sure that from Bishop W. A. Patterson Sr. was pretty much the same. I'm sure he got that knowledge from him. The radio station WBBP (1480 AM) was created by Bishop G. E. Patterson. It's still in operation and can be accessed online. I'm not sure if Bountiful Blessings Incorporated still runs it, because I've been gone from Memphis since 1995. I know Bishop G. E. Patterson also had a record label for a while. Podium Records' first project was "Bishop G. E. Patterson Presents: Rance Allen and the Soul Winner's Conference Choir." The project was nominated for a Grammy Award in 1999. There are two organizations that my uncle was affiliated with. There's the Temple of Deliverance and then there's Bountiful Blessings Incorporated. I'm not sure what falls to whom or where.

CHAPTER 10: THE PATTERSON FAMILY

Now the COGIC ministry is available online and thousands of people all over the world are still listening to sermons from the Patterson family members, especially Bishop G. E. Patterson. It feels awesome. I love it when I get on social media and scroll around and come across someone who has uploaded a snippet of a sermon or something to that effect.

It makes me very happy. I always make sure I put love on the post, whether it be Facebook, Instagram or whatever. It's a great tribute to the legacy and just his awesomeness. I also like to read through the comments. They say that he (G.E.) was a great voice and that he is greatly missed. I agree.

I'm still moved even when I see old video footage of Big Dad, Bishop W. A. Patterson. There is one video that comes to mind. In his older age when he was asked to get up and speak during a service, people would think that because he was so frail, he was barely going to be able to get ten words out.

Then by the time 10 minutes was over, he had everybody up on their feet. He was so fiery, and they would say: "Wait a minute. How did he go from barely looking like he's sitting in a chair to preaching you into a tizzy!"

Bishop W.A. Patterson Sr. & Bishop G.E. Patterson

Of course, Bishop G. E. Patterson had that same thing that he could do. There was another time when Big Dad got up to make remarks and my uncle G. E. put his arm around Big Dad's shoulders to signal that it was time for him to go ahead and sit down. Then just as he touched them, Uncle G. E. got happy (as in the Holy Ghost).

The first time I saw the video of this it was right after Big Dad had died. We were at the convocation in Memphis, and my sister and I were sitting next to each other. When he came up on the screen, we grabbed each other, oh my God, we laughed, and we cried. It was a very powerful moment.

I'm glad that Logan has been able to pull together this book and for documenting our history of Black excellence. It's good for our family legacy and lineage. We need to get these stories out there and to have it told, because a lot of people don't know all the contributions that our parents and our grandparents have made.

We don't brag on ourselves. When I listen to what Logan and his wife have done, a lot of people don't know those stories and so forth. So, it's nice to know that someone is trying to make sure that there is a written history of all of our accomplishments. I think it's great.

Internationally, COGIC can be found in more than 100 nations. Its worldwide membership is estimated to be between six and eight million, composing more than 25,000 congregations throughout the world. The geographical dioceses of the denomination are called "jurisdictions." Currently there are over three hundred jurisdictions.

CHAPTER 10: THE PATTERSON FAMILY

More memories of Bishop G. E. Patterson from Dr. Logan H. Westbrooks

Gilbert and I were schoolmates and playmates along with Jim Neely. I also remember Bishop Gilbert Patterson's sisters Mary Patterson, Lee Ella Patterson Smith, and Barbara Patterson.

Mary is the mother of Milton Hawkins, pastor of Gilbert's old church Temple of Deliverance.

Bishop Milton R. Hawkins, Pastor of Temple of Deliverance in Memphis, TN, and the Jurisdictional Prelate of the Guatemala Ecclesiastical Jurisdiction.

Incidentally, the Temple of Deliverance church is now located at 369 G.E. Patterson Avenue in Memphis. Talk about a full circle Patterson legacy fulfilled.

Lee Ella Patterson Smith & Bishop Samuel Smith, Founder of Southside Church of God in Christ

Lee Ella Patterson Smith married Bishop Samuel Smith, my friend and mentor. Lee Ella attended LeMoyne-Owen College, and she taught school.

She had two daughters. I always spent 100% of my time with Lee Ella and Bishop Smith during the Convocations in November. I was also his driver, and we attended all events together. Bishop Smith passed in 2004 and Lee Ella passed away in 2011.

Barbara Patterson is the youngest and she is my age. Barbara was also a close friend of Lulah McEwen. Lulah was the daughter of Bishop A.

B. McEwen Sr. and Sammie Martin McEwen. Bishop McEwen was appointed overseer of the Church of God in Christ from 1922 to 1954. Lulah became the renown Dr. Lulah Hedgeman. She gained nationwide acclaim for directing the choral music department at Overton High School, winning first place in all competitions for twenty years.

All of the Patterson children were also musically inclined. They sang and played piano. The father, Elder W. A. Patterson, was the pastor of Holy Temple COGIC located on Wilson Street in South Memphis.

The family moved to Detroit when Gilbert had completed sixth grade. Gilbert and I had the same sixth grade teacher, Mrs. Broadnax, and we both stayed in touch with her through the years.

Mrs. Gladys Greene Broadnax, teacher in the Memphis Schools. Passed away Jan 14, 2018 at 97 years old.

Bishop Milton Hawkins is the son of Mary Patterson. He is now the pastor of Bountiful Blessings Temple of Deliverance COGIC. He followed in the footsteps of his uncle Gilbert Earl Patterson, who was the founder of the church.

Gilbert returned to Memphis to become the pastor of Holy Temple, his father's church. Of course, Gilbert later became the presiding bishop of the Church of God in Christ in 2000 at age sixty, making him the youngest person to ever be elected as presiding bishop.

Gilbert Patterson Jr. passed away on March 20, 2007. He was sixty-seven. The U.S. Senate passed a resolution in his honor on March 28 of the same year. At one point his radio and TV ministry reached over 15 million people.

My work in the record industry has received more publicity than my work in the ministry. However, I am quite proud of my foundations in the Church of God in Christ. I am a third-generation member of COGIC. When you include my siblings, our family is five generations strong in the Church of God in Christ.

I accepted the call to the ministry under the leadership of Benjamin Crouch at Christ Memorial COGIC in Los Angeles. I eventually became a pastor and was ordained in 1996 by Bishop Bernard Hackworth. I was later appointed Secretary of the Metropolitan Jurisdiction of Southern California, and I had previously served as the director of Public Relations.

In the year 2000 I was a candidate for the Trustee Board and ran on a platform that called for annual audits of the national church, mandatory financial training and investment workshops for new pastors and the creation of educational incentives for members of the church among many other initiatives.

Elder Westbrooks poses with General Board member Bishop S. L. Green, as he solicits his support for the board of trustees.

CHAPTER 10: THE PATTERSON FAMILY

Through my exposure to the church over the years, I was blessed to have firsthand examples of outstanding leadership, dutiful stewardship, and a vision for an ever growing and ever evolving body of Christ.

This lifelong relationship with the church has left an indelible impact on me. The Patterson family is a huge part of this connectivity. For that I am eternally grateful.

Westbrooks announces his candidacy while his Jurisdidtional Bishop, J. Bernard Hackworth looks on, with Bishop Chandler D. Owen, and Bishop J.N. Haynes

Westbrooks announces his candidacy while his Jurisdictional Bishop J. Bernard Hackworth looks on, with Bishop Chandler D. Owen, and Bishop J. N. Haynes
Photo: COGIC Times
Vol. 2 Nov 7–14, 2000

Elder Westbrooks poses with General Board member, Bishop S. L. Green, as he solicits his support for the board of trustees.

Photo: COGIC Times Vol. 2 Nov. 7–14, 2000

CHAPTER 11

THE STILES KATOE FAMILY

*Memories of the Stiles Family from
Dorothy Stiles Katoe*

I am Dorothy Kathleen Stiles, and my married name is Katoe. We lived at 1492 McMillan Street in the Lauderdale Sub.

Ellen Louise Dunford Stiles Sept 30, 1910–Jan 1, 2009

CHAPTER 11: THE STILES KATOE FAMILY

My mother was Mrs. Ellen Stiles. My brothers and sisters were Allen, Evelyn, Sheila, Mary, and Saint James II. Also, at that time, I had an Aunt Kathleen Dunford, who lived there with her daughter, Lula Patricia Dunford Crawford. And if I'm not mistaken, I also had another aunt who lived there for a while with her son. And that was Mrs. Evelyn McDonald, and her son, Henry McDonald.

My mother was a schoolteacher in the city school system and my father (who did not live with us most of that time) worked at the Memphis Country Club.

Mom earned her degree from Tennessee State University, formerly known as Tennessee College of Agriculture & Industry. She dedicated 31 years as an educator. Over the course of her remarkable ninety-eight years, she was deeply involved in her community. She was a proud member of Sigma Gamma Rho Sorority, Inc., the National Association for the Advancement of Colored People (NAACP), the Soulsville Neighborhood Watch Association, and the Loving and Lifting Caregivers Support Ministry at Saint Andrew African Methodist Episcopal Church. My mother also generously gave her time as a volunteer for the American Heart Association. Her faith was central to her life, and she remained an active and devoted member of Saint Augustine Catholic Church.

I attended Saint Augustine Catholic School for all of the grades one through twelve. I graduated in 1956. I also attended Saint Augustine Catholic Church. For my higher education, I attended LeMoyne-Owen College, and I graduated in 1960 with a degree in education and liberal arts.

We did not own a vehicle. We rode the bus most of the time or we got a ride with someone. There was a sense of unity in the community. I recall, almost everyone knew everybody. We were friends. When we were younger, we played together. We were able to go to each other's homes and visit each other.

As youngsters we were not aware of any political unrest during that time. My family lived in the area and did their thing. The Whites who lived in the area did their thing. Of course, at that time, we who lived south of Parkway were Black and north of Parkway is where the Whites lived.

The schools that we went to were sort of out of the area. We went to a parochial Catholic school. As I mentioned, we did not have a car. So, we walked or rode the bus to the school, which was a little distance. We did not mind walking. It was no problem and most of my friends or neighbors went to the public schools there. I don't recall any other person going to Saint Augustine in that area besides my family. If I remember correctly, when I was in high school was when they had the bus boycott that was started by Rosa Parks.

We didn't ride the bus at any time during that time. We had to walk downtown. We had to walk anywhere that we had to go. Of course, we weren't too bothered about it because it was for a just cause. Everybody was committed to that cause. I'm sure parents who had to get work at a distance encountered an issue, but the people worked together and helped each other out. That was the main issue that I recall during that time.

Over the years we have had high achievers to come from that area. I know Logan Westbrooks and his family came from the area. Most of them became well respected and had high achieving occupations. Many people who came out of that area were educators. A few people had businesses as they got older.

As I was growing up as a very young child, I would say that it was sort of a poor neighborhood. We did not have much, but the families had aspirations and wanted more for their families. And as I stated, some became educators, and some had businesses, some became self-employed or started their own careers. I remember the Davenports, the Neelys, of course I said the Westbrooks. I also remember the leaders of Shiloh Baptist Church.

CHAPTER 11: THE STILES KATOE FAMILY

In our neighborhood our families seemed to love each other. We cared for each other. We also aspired for the best in our families. I don't recall very much violence during that time, however I'm sure there was some. There may have been disagreements or fights, but eventually they made up and everybody got along.

CHAPTER 12

THE WEAVER HOWARD FAMILY

Memories of the Howard Weaver family from Alonzo Weaver III

Alonzo Weaver III

I spent time in Lauderdale Sub as a kid although I never lived there, but my oldest sister did until my parents bought their own house. That house was built on Wilson Street outside of Lauderdale Sub. When my family lived in Lauderdale Sub the first house was at 1579 Lauderdale, which was the house of my grandparents Simon L. Howard, and Magnolia Davenport Howard.

CHAPTER 12: THE WEAVER HOWARD FAMILY

For a short period of time, it was the residence of my parents Alonzo Weaver and Claribelle Howard Weaver. They had their first child, a daughter (Phoebe Weaver Williams) who lived there for a short period of time until they built their house off of South Parkway. The second address is 1826 Lauderdale, which was the home of my grandmother Magnolia Howard. She lived there after she divorced my grandfather Simon Howard.

The first home at 1579 Lauderdale was the home of Simon L. Howard and Magnolia Davenport. Magnolia who was the daughter of Virginia Hawkins Davenport and Jake Davenport. Simon Howard Sr. was my grandfather, and I am not sure when he built that house. I know that he raised his children there. They were Claribelle Howard (my mother), my Uncle Simon L. Howard Jr. and my aunt Emma Howard Scott. Those are those are the children who grew up there. As they got older, they all went out on their own.

Alonzo Weaver II and Claribelle Weaver
Photo: Weaver family.

My mother married my father during World War II or sometime in that era. They had a daughter named Phoebe, who lived there with them for a period of time. They lived at 1579 Lauderdale until my parents moved to a house that they built in another part of the city.

My grandfather Simon Howard worked for the Frisco Railroad as a porter. My grandmother Magnolia Davenport Howard was a schoolteacher. She taught at Orleans School at one time but I'm not sure what other schools where she may have taught. She may have possibly taught at Lincoln.

My mother Claribelle Howard was a librarian. She taught school and then became a librarian at Mitchell High School, then ultimately, she worked at Southside High School until she retired.

Simon Howard Jr. 1923–2017

Simon Jr. worked for the post office. He started out as a letter carrier and moved up into management at the post office. My aunt Emma D was also a schoolteacher, I don't remember the school.

CHAPTER 12: THE WEAVER HOWARD FAMILY

She moved to Atlanta, got married and had a child named Frank. She married Frank Scott. My parents and my older sister moved from 1579 Lauderdale to 1380 Wilson Street, which is outside of Lauderdale Sub.

1826 Lauderdale is where I actually spent time with my grandmother there. It was, particularly during the Civil Rights era. It was a time when they were having various protests and I stayed there with her. I also stayed with her a lot during the summer. Mostly what she did for me that I will always remember is that she taught me how to read music. Eventually I learned how to play the piano myself. So, I'm not that great of a piano player, but I did learn how to read music from my grandmother. She was trying to find something to occupy my time during the summers. The family was musical. My grandmother played piano, and my mother played piano. My aunt played the piano. My uncle played a little bit, but he didn't stay with it.

During the Civil Rights era there were things that were called Black Mondays. I think they had to do with teachers and the teachers' strike. Black Monday centered on education. That was also, of course, the time when Martin Luther King was assassinated. I didn't stay there then.

My grandmother was always very much a part of my life as far as making sure that we got home from school okay, and that sort of thing. That was one key thing.

There were several other things that as a little kid, it doesn't really register with you, but my grandmother never drove. She got around on public transportation. She took the bus, and I was her little side kick. We would go downtown going shopping and then come back to 1826 Lauderdale on what was the Number 13 Lauderdale bus. She was very capable of getting around the city to where she needed to go using public transportation. As a little kid who was growing up in the car culture, that was kind of different.

I would know if my grandmother was coming over and we'd be looking forward to it. When we lived on Wilson Street I would see her getting off the bus. She'd have her shopping bags with her and cross the street. I was kind of amazed by all that. She was very independent.

My grandfather was a member of Morning View Missionary Baptist Church on Carnegie Street in the Lauderdale sub. My mother, father and my grandmother Magnolia were members of Avery Chapel which is over near the Soulsville area. I don't think it was called Soulsville back then. I'm not sure what it was called then. It was Trigg and Saxon Streets near LeMoyne-Owen College.

My mom started playing for churches when she was like 17 years old. She played for Morning View. I believe she played for the Church of God in Christ that was in that area. My father was also a member of Morning View and several of the Davenports. My grandfather was a Howard. You can probably get that lineage from some of the others.

I would say that our family always valued respect. I would say that they considered that to be important. I'll tell you a story. I had an observation when I was kid. Back then Lauderdale Sub was kind of diverse and my grandmother was good friends with Miss Frances Keeney, who had a grocery store in the area.

The store was on Lauderdale. My grandmother had a good relationship with her. That was one of the things that I saw with my grandmother. She formed deep and lasting relationships with lasting friendships. That was very important.

The family also valued education and music. My grandmother and my mom were both graduates. I remember going to my grandmother's graduation from University of Memphis when she got her masters. My mother and my grandmother got their masters from the University of Memphis.

CHAPTER 12: THE WEAVER HOWARD FAMILY

I am presently the senior vice president and chief operating officer for Memphis Light, Gas and Water, which is a three-service municipal utility located here in Memphis, Tennessee. We serve all of Shelby County with electric and gas, and most of Shelby County with water. It is the largest three-service utility and it's a $1.2 billion enterprise. I've been there for now thirty-nine-and-a-half years. It will be my fortieth year in June (2023). I have been blessed to be there and have had a great career there.

I grew up in Memphis and I graduated from Hamilton High School. When I finished high school, I went to Rensselaer Polytechnic Institute to get my Bachelors of Science in Mechanical Engineering. Then I came to work for Memphis Light. Gas and Water. During the summers, I worked as an intern at MLGW. Then I got my master's in business administration in 1997 from University of Memphis.

I've had various roles at Memphis Light, Gas and Water. I've been a manager of Electric Operations, the vice president of Operations, vice president of Engineering, vice president of Customer Operations, vice president of Engineering Operations, and now I'm in the senior VP, Chief Operating Officer position, which has all the Electric Gas and Water engineering and the electric, gas and water construction along with the gas purchasing.

So, I've got a hefty amount of responsibility with about 1,500 employees out of the 2,700 that are with MLGW that report in that chain.

Simon L. Howard was a Black man in the segregated South who worked on the railroad back in those days. I don't think that he ever thought in a million years that his grandson would be the SVP and COO of Memphis Light Gas and Water. I don't think that he would have thought that at all. Back then, they were just fighting for their jobs at the Frisco Railroads. It was during the same time of Asa Philip Randolph (founder of the Brotherhood of Sleeping Car Porters) and the Pullman Porters.

Memories of the Weaver Howard family from Phoebe Weaver Williams

Phoebe Weaver Williams

I am Phoebe Weaver Williams. The home that I resided in as a child was located at 1579 South Lauderdale.

I was born in 1946 so I would estimate that my parents probably lived there at the time of my birth. I know my mother and dad (Claribelle Howard Weaver and Alonzo Weaver II.) had both traveled from Chicago and arrived in Memphis and stayed with my grandmother and grandfather (Magnolia Davenport Howard and Simon Howard). So that would have been for me from 1946, and I think until I was about age eight or nine, which would have been 1954 and this is the estimated time frame that I actually lived there. I'm not exactly sure of the ending date.

CHAPTER 12: THE WEAVER HOWARD FAMILY

My siblings were not born until after I left Lauderdale Sub. I'm eight years older than my sister and fifteen years older than my brother. It would have been me and my parents at the time of my birth until maybe age six or so. Then my parents moved out and built a home.

I stayed with my grandmother (Magnolia Davenport Howard) because my parents were working and teaching in schools located in Shelby County, and they didn't have a car to get to work. So, they had to ride with people. It was just too much for them to have to find someone to care for me and manage to get to their jobs. So, I stayed with my grandmother until my parents eventually purchased a car.

My mother Claribelle Howard Weaver was a librarian at Southside High School and my father was a principal at Mitchell Road High School at the end of his career. Earlier in his career, he was a teacher before he became a principal. So, at the time, we were all living at 1579 Lauderdale he may not have entered the occupation of teaching.

For the last 18 years of his career as an educator, he was a principal at Mitchell Road High School. Before then, he was a teacher. I know he taught at Ford Road School and I forgot the other schools where he may have taught.

Before he entered teaching, he may have had other types of jobs, because after I was born that was the end of World War II and there were many soldiers who had returned. There was a shortage of housing, and so I don't believe he entered teaching immediately after the war. My father served in World War II. He was a veteran. I believe his classification when he was discharged was known as a Warrant Officer.

My first grade school was Lutheran Cooperative, which was a small Lutheran church school. At the time I was going to school, the schools were segregated. It was a small Lutheran school for Black children. I attended Lutheran Cooperative probably until the fourth or fifth grade. Then by the sixth grade, I stayed with my parents and then I attended

Hamilton Elementary and Hamilton High School. I never attended Lincoln Elementary, but I'm certainly familiar with it because my grandmother taught at Lincoln Elementary. She also taught at Lutheran Cooperative School. I think after she left Lutheran Cooperative, she started teaching at Lincoln Elementary School.

Mrs. Magnolia Howard

Services for Mrs. Magnolia Davenport Howard, 76, of 1826 South Lauderdale, widow of Simon Howard, will be at 1 p.m. tomorrow at T. H. Hayes & Sons Funeral Home with burial in Elmwood. Mrs. Howard, a retired teacher, died Saturday at her home.

Funeral announcement for Mrs. Magnolia Howard

Walter Guy Hawkins and Willie Gertrude Hawkins

CHAPTER 12: THE WEAVER HOWARD FAMILY

My maternal grandmother was Magnolia Davenport Howard. Her mother (my great grandmother) was Virginia Hawkins Davenport. Her brother was Walter Hawkins Sr. and he was referred to as Uncle Bud.

His wife was Willie G. Hawkins. I remember visiting with Uncle Bud and Aunt Willie. They eventually lived at 1658 Carnegie Street.

Well, if I recall what my mother explained, my parents lived in more than one home growing up as children on Lauderdale. So, the homes were progressively better and nicer. I think the first home they lived in was probably within a couple of blocks from 1579 Lauderdale, but perhaps going North.

I don't remember the exact address but it's probably a vacant lot now. My family lived in at least a couple of homes before they moved to 1579 South Lauderdale.

By the time my grandmother moved to 1826 South Lauderdale, my mother and her siblings had their own home. So, they wouldn't have grown up in 1826 South Lauderdale. I stayed in Lauderdale Sub after my parents moved to a family home on 1380 Wilson Street. It's on the South side of Memphis and within walking distance of Hamilton School. I believe I was probably eight or nine when I left 1579 South Lauderdale. I was born in 1946, so I remember in 1954 I was staying at 1380 Wilson Street.

The main reason why I remember that is because Brown versus The Board of Education was decided in 1954 and I can remember seeing my father coming home after that decision in the newspaper. So, for sure I was living at 1380 Wilson Street at the time by 1954. My father was very happy about the decision because that decision struck down racial segregation in the schools and deemed it as unconstitutional. He shared his happiness with me and explained to me what the decision meant.

My grandmother was a member of Avery Chapel African Methodist Episcopal Church, which at the time was not on Trigg Street. It was at a different address. It was one of the oldest churches in the city of Memphis. It eventually moved to Trigg but before that it was located at a different address more towards downtown. So, Avery Chapel was my grandmother's church. She was AME (African Methodist Episcopal). My grandfather Simon L. Howard Sr. was Baptist. He belonged to Morning View Baptist Church, which is located in the Lauderdale Subdivision. My grandfather's son is Simon L. Howard Jr.

My chosen career eventually became law. Initially, I graduated from Hamilton High School. I attended college and after college for about 10 years. I then worked for the Social Security Administration. I started as a Claims Representative and worked my way up the ladder to a become a manager of a branch office.

But in 1978 I left the Social Security Administration because I wanted to become a lawyer. I wanted to go to law school. I finished Marquette University Law School in 1981. After graduation I practiced for about four and a half to five years as a lawyer representing management with a law firm in Milwaukee, Wisconsin. While practicing law, there was an opportunity to teach at Marquette University Law School. I was hired to work at Marquette University Law School as a Law professor, and I worked there until my retirement in 2014.

When thinking of the essence of the Memphis Lauderdale community, as a child I recall a heavy emphasis on education because my grandmother Magnolia Howard was an elementary school teacher. I think she taught first grade. She often prepared exercises in math and reading for her first graders. She was also taking care of me.

Even when I was four and five years old she gave me math and reading problems to work. Thanks to her teaching, by the time I entered kindergarten at Lutheran Cooperative they placed me in first grade at age five.

I got a little earlier start than most children who normally start first grade at age six because they felt that I could do the work. They didn't have the same age restrictions in the small little private Lutheran school that they had in the public schools regarding a child being an appropriate age before they can enter a certain grade.

There was a heavy emphasis on education. My grandmother was valedictorian of her high school class. She was always interested in advancing her own education. Over the years, I saw my grandmother take courses at LeMoyne. She eventually graduated from Rust College or the Mississippi Industrial College. I think the two were close together and she eventually earned her bachelor's degree. My mother earned her bachelor's degree from Lemoyne-Owen College. That's where she met my dad. He earned his bachelor's degree at LeMoyne-Owen College as well.

Growing up over the years with teachers in the family meant that my father and mother would go to many graduation ceremonies at LeMoyne-Owen College, and I was with them. Their former students had completed college and both of my parents pursued master's degrees after their bachelor's degrees while I was growing up. I would say that there was definitely a rich tradition of learning, of doing well in school, of advancing your education, and just reading and acquiring more knowledge in general.

I don't remember too many explicit conversations about how to overcome adversity. It was more about the examples they set. The examples we had are to focus on your mission. What are your goals? What is it you have to do? Keep your focus on the goals that you want to accomplish, rather than focusing on the impediments that are in your way.

For example, growing up there were segregated public libraries. So, I knew I couldn't go to the large, impressive library in Memphis where only Whites were allowed to go. But I could go to the library for Colored children. My father took me to the library to check out books and he knew the librarians. They were really kind and nice to me.

I checked out books and developed my interest in reading, travel, and places I wanted to go. I think that's where I first read books about Hawaii. I was fascinated. I remember as a child I read more than one book about Hawaii and I really wanted to visit Hawaii one day.

It wasn't until I was fifty years old that I actually visited Hawaii. It planted seeds of me wanting to travel and wanting to have new experiences and to experience different cultures.

So, I would say that one of the main examples I observed was that with my grandmother and my grandfather, everybody had a mission that they were on as far as what they wanted to accomplish in life. Yes, there were things going around us that sent messages. You had to use the Colored drinking fountain. You couldn't go in certain restaurants because you were Black. There was not a whole lot of conversation about what we couldn't do. There was more conversation about what we were expected to do.

I had some wonderful childhood experiences that I recall in the Lauderdale Sub. Magnolia Davenport Matthews also shared memories of the Lauderdale Sub. She's a second cousin to me. She's my mother's first cousin. The family's name for her is Sweet Baby. I remember that whole family. They're older than I am, but as a little child, I was just fascinated with them and wanted to be around them. They used to walk over and pick me up when I was the only child at the home of my grandmother and grandfather, and my mother and father.

I was so excited to be with them because there were several of them and I just loved being with them as a child. I always had fond memories

CHAPTER 12: THE WEAVER HOWARD FAMILY

of being able to follow my cousins around. They were always nice and sweet to me. I just have fond memories of my experiences living in the Lauderdale Sub.

Fortunately, my sisters joined a church that engaged in a lot of travel experiences. So, I've been able to travel with them. The first trip was to Israel and Egypt. Then we went to South Africa, and Brazil, the Greek Isles, China, and Hawaii twice. That was with that group.

I had an opportunity to go to London and Paris through my work. I was giving a presentation in the UK at one of the law schools there. I also took a side trip to Paris with that experience. I taught for about six weeks in the summer in Australia at a law school and Australia. We had an exchange program between Marquette and the law school and one of the law schools in Australia. I taught there for five weeks in the city of Brisbane. That was a really interesting experience. On the way home, I went to New Zealand and spent time on the North Island. I visited Auckland and areas around the North Island. But with the church group, I also went back to New Zealand and Australia and had a chance to visit Sydney in Melbourne and a number of places in New Zealand because it was a cruise where we stopped at various places.

I'm a parent. I have two daughters and my oldest daughter particularly loves to travel. She's been everywhere. She and her husband and my grandchild have been to Japan, Paris, and Spain. Even in high school, she went to Costa Rica as an AFS (American Field Service) student, because early on she wanted to travel. She attended a Montessori school. Her teacher was from France. So, at age thirteen she had a passport because her teacher was from Alsace, France and she was also teaching them French.

She took about thirteen of her students to Alsace, which is on the border of France and Germany. So, my oldest daughter was bitten by the travel bug at a very young age. As a result, she's traveled all over. She loved to learn languages. During high school she studied French and German and then while she was in Costa Rica, she learned Spanish. She went on a foreign study experience while she was in college to Senegal, where she learned Wolof. So, she learned to speak several different languages and she still travels a lot.

CHAPTER 13

THE WESTBROOKS FAMILY

*Shirley Westbrooks shares memories of
The Westbrooks family from the Lauderdale Sub*

Shirley Westbrooks Smith

I am Shirley Westbrooks Smith. We lived at 1500 Carnegie Street in Memphis, Tennessee. I don't know the zip code, there were no zips at that time. I believe that we moved there in the summer of July 1946. We lived there about six and a half years. We moved in October of 1953. I believe that was the year because I had just finished high school.

Al Jr., Logan, Alphonso Sr., Shirley and Pearl Westbrooks

My father was Alphonso Westbrooks Sr. My mother was Erma Bowen Westbrooks and there were five children: Alphonso Westbrooks Jr., Shirley Westbrooks (currently Shirley Westbrooks Smith), Pearl Westbrooks (Hines), Logan Westbrooks, and my younger sister Gloria Westbrooks (Moore).

Logan and Gloria Westbrooks in front of 1500 Carnegie Street

CHAPTER 13: THE WESTBROOKS FAMILY

When we moved to Carnegie Street I was entering sixth grade. I attended Lincoln Elementary School and I remember Miss Diamond was the teacher. In fact, she taught sixth grade and eighth grade. All of us entered Lincoln School that fall, except for Gloria because she was just a baby. She was born in 1945 so she was just a year old. Logan, Alphonso, Pearl, and Shirley entered Lincoln School in the fall of 1946.

As I said, I was in sixth grade. It was a new experience because it was a very small school. It only had eight or nine teachers because there was just one teacher for each grade, plus the principal and the building engineer, who was called the custodian at that time. I attended Lincoln from the sixth through eighth grade. In the seventh grade, I had a male teacher. That was my first time experiencing a male teacher. He was a very good teacher. His name was James Taylor. The next year, I was in eighth grade and Miss Diamond was back. She taught me for two years in the sixth grade and eighth grade. I graduated that spring from Lincoln as the valedictorian of the class and it was a good year.

Lincoln School Park

I met a lot of new people, some of them have remained friends until this day. Later we all went to Booker T. Washington High School that fall together. I'd say that it was thirty or forty of us in that class. I'll say thirty-five, just taking a wild guess. I have a picture of the entire class. Lincoln Elementary was on Orleans Street, four or five streets from where we lived.

Then we went on to Booker T. Washington High School. There were no junior high schools during that time. It was just elementary and high school, no middle schools or any of that.

Elementary school was from grades one through eight. There were no kindergartens. You had to do that on your own. When we went to Lincoln, I was in the sixth grade. I believe Logan was in the fourth grade, Pearl was in the second, and Alphonso Jr, my older brother must have been in the seventh grade when we moved to Carnegie Street.

Shirley and Pearl Westbrooks, 1948

Prior to Lincoln, we attended Porter school. We were living in LeMoyne Gardens at that time. We moved from LeMoyne Gardens to Carnegie

Street in the summer of 1946. So, the first five years I spent at Porter. All four of us had attended Porter up until 1946.

I graduated from Booker T. in the spring of 1953. In the fall we moved to Latham Street. There were some very good teachers at Booker T. Washington High School. It was a four-year school with grades nine through twelve.

After graduating from Booker T Washington, I attended LeMoyne-Owen College, which is a local college here in the city of Memphis. I attended there for four years.

During those four years, I made more new friends. Some of them are lifelong. Most of them have gone on to glory, but a few are still alive. Several of us were initiated into Alpha Kappa Alpha Sorority.

I majored in sociology because at that time, I wanted to become a social worker. I changed my mind and ended up being a teacher. I taught school for 31 years in Memphis, Tennessee. I taught junior high school because when I first started teaching in 1957, schools were still divided into elementary and high school. In around 1961 the city of Memphis changed the breakdown of the schools from grades one through eight for elementary schools, to grades one through six. Then they came up with Junior High school and Junior High was grades seven through nine and then there was Senior High school, which was grades ten through twelve.

I taught fifth grade at Riverview Elementary for three years. Then I got married. Shortly after that, I had a baby. After the maternity leave ended, I was assigned to a junior high school and I taught seventh grade Social Studies and American History. Later I also taught Civics. I also taught at Porter (which became a Jr. High School) for quite a number of years, like ten or fifteen years.

Along came integration and busing. During that time all of the faculty all over the city had to be integrated. Many of the teachers were transferred to other schools and busing was put into play. I was transferred to Melrose Junior High school. And I taught the same subjects at Melrose as I did at Porter.

Then a few years later, this was Plan A. I don't know why they labeled these things like that, but they did. A few years later they came up with Plan Z. In Plan Z they changed the elementary school set up and they changed the faculties also. If it was a dominant White school, it (the faculty) had to be 40% Black and 60% White. If it was a predominantly Black school, then the percentages were reversed. It was a complicated situation. Then from there I went to Graceland Junior High School, and I stayed there until that retired and I retired in 1988.

While growing up in Lauderdale Sub my dad had a vehicle for as long as I can remember. The cars gradually got better. At first there was the type of car that we call "hoopties" but as time went on, we went to real nice cars. He would start buying new cars or slightly used cars. He didn't go to the junkyard, but he always owned a car in his profession.

Alphonso Westbrooks Sr. and Charles Bowen in front of Memphis World newspaper.

CHAPTER 13: THE WESTBROOKS FAMILY

He (my dad) was a circulation manager for the *Memphis World* newspaper, which was owned by the Scott family. That was a Black-owned paper in the city. They also published the Atlanta Daily World and The Birmingham World.

It was my father's job to get papers to the carriers, the newspaper boys. He had to go all over the city of Memphis. He also went into West Memphis, Arkansas, and places like that delivering papers to the carriers. Then he had to go back and collect his money. Once we went to Porter school, he would drive us to school practically every morning. If the weather was bad, he would come back and get us that evening.

We only went to one church. There was only one church of each denomination in the neighborhood. Our church was the Carnegie Church of God in Christ, but there was one Baptist church if I can recall. It was the Morning View Baptist Church, which I remember was up close to the 1600 block of Carnegie near where the Hawkins family lived. There was a Methodist Church. I don't remember the name but that was a Methodist Church in the area. Of course, the Church of God in Christ (COGIC), which was referred to as the sanctified church. It was, it was not quite on the corner, but it was on Carnegie. That was our church.

Carnegie Church of God in Christ, circa 1940s

At Carnegie COGIC we went to Bible school and Sunday school, all at that one little wooden church. We went there from the time of my birth until I was about twelve or thirteen years old.

Once we moved, we stayed there quite a few years until I finished eighth grade. Then, the whole family moved its membership from Carnegie COGIC to the Temple Church of God in Christ. It was located at Lauderdale and Georgia Avenue. So, then we would spend our time between the two churches through the week. We went to Tuesday night service and Wednesday night Bible study at Carnegie Church of God in Christ. Then for Sunday service and choir rehearsal, we would go to the Temple Church of God in Christ. So, for a minute we went to two churches. They really wanted us to be religious.

That's where I met the Hawkins family at Carnegie Church of God in Christ. Elder Robert McNeal Sr. was the pastor. He was a nice man. He was one of those "Read on" preachers. Let me tell you about the "read on" preachers.

What would happen was, the preacher would have a reader to read the scripture during his sermon. Usually it was his wife, but not always. Remember that back in the 1940s and early 50s, older Black people were not very literate. They didn't go to school but maybe one or two years or not at all. They worked on the farms. There were a lot of rural areas even in Memphis during that time. So, it's quite possible that the pastor couldn't read very well. This applied to most of the sanctified preachers at that time. They would get a good reader in the congregation to read the Bible for them.

They would choose a scripture and tell the reader; "Read." And she would read a few chapters or a few verses and then he (the preacher) would expound on them as he interpreted them. Then he would say "Read on." Then she would read a few more lines, and they were called the "Read on" preachers. What most people didn't know is that they were carried on that way because they couldn't read so they wanted somebody else to read for them.

There was a cookie factory on Lauderdale Street. The cookie aroma would just flood the neighborhood. I remember it as we would go to school. We were going to Booker T. Washington High School at this time, and we'd save our lunch money. We wouldn't have but a nickel or a dime, but we would save our lunch money so that we could stop at the cookie factory on our way home and get a bag of cookies. And they would sell a bag of cookies for a nickel. It's unheard of today and they were big cookies not like these little cookies that you buy now. Some days they would run out of cookies. Talk about being hurt! You would look forward to eating those cookies then you'd get there, and they would have sold out. The cookies were broken cookies that they did not sell to their regular customers. But anyway, that's where the cookie factory was. I believe it was Dortch's Cookie Company. So that was one of the highlights.

Old cookie factory on Lauderdale Street

There was Lynn's Donut shop also. It was on Parkway Street between Lauderdale and Carnegie. We loved to go there to purchase donuts. It was a grocery store there also, and I remember that Logan got a job at the grocery store delivering groceries. They say what goes around comes around.

Back in that day people would go to the grocery store, pick out their groceries and then there were always some grocery boys there with a bicycle and a basket on the bicycle. You put the groceries in the basket, and then the boy delivered it to your house. That's what Logan did. He would deliver groceries to people's houses. I don't know what he was paid. Sometimes people would give him tips, and the grocer would pay him a small amount of money for delivering and working for them, because he was actually working for the grocery store. Another thing was the grocery stores in the neighborhood would allow people to charge their groceries. We didn't ever do very much charging groceries. Charging means paying on credit.

Since my dad was the circulation manager for the newspaper, people would pay him something every day and we would use that to get our groceries. Each store had their own delivery people. So, that has come back around but in a more sophisticated manner. Now we have Instacart and Amazon. They have the same kind of thing now, except you can order online and they bring it to your house.

Of course, back then they also had live chickens! They would be in a little coop in front, and you'd choose one. I don't remember how people got those live chickens home, but I know they'd take them home and kill them. It was horrible. I remember my dad would kill the chicken. My mom would pick the feathers off and cut it up and cook it. You don't want to eat that chicken.

As for the atmosphere of the people in the neighborhood, I would just say that they were just happy, happy Black people for that day in time.

CHAPTER 13: THE WESTBROOKS FAMILY

Everybody looked out for each other. There weren't a lot of professionals, but during that period of time in Black neighborhoods there was no distinction. Now in some areas where you live, only certain classes of people live in that area. Back then it was mixed.

A preacher might live two doors up from where you lived. The pastors and the preachers were always respected in the neighborhood. Then the teachers would live across the street. Then the maids would be a door or two away from you and the drunkard would be somewhere on the street. Everybody knew which house it was where he lived.

We had a wealth of professions. Or course, Black people worked in the department stores as the maids and elevator operators, which were considered good jobs in that period of time. Everybody lived together. Nobody lived on one side of town versus the other. There was no class distinction is what I should say, because everybody mingled. We lived close together. We went to the same churches, attended the same fish fries on Friday night and just enjoyed each other's company.

We are still living back in the 1940s. Racism during the 1940s was supposed to be separate but equal, but it was everything but that. Black people had not really started rebelling. Although they were aware of the differences, they had not reached a point where they would fight against it.

There was some police brutality during that time. They discussed it. They talked about it but there was not much that Black people could do or thought that they could do during this time. I'll go back to Lauderdale Sub, because that's what we're talking about. Lauderdale Sub are the streets up to the south of Waldorf all the way up to Person Street. Black people resided there.

Going north on Lauderdale from Waldorf was White. Caucasians resided there. Lauderdale and Waldorf was a dividing line. Everybody on one side was Black and everybody on the other side was White.

Then in the other direction east and west, I believe the dividing line was Latham Street.

Then we go in the other direction, and you get over to a street called Webb, but it was out of Lauderdale Sub. This was the block in which most Black families lived. Outside of that area were White folks. There were a few streets in between where one side of the street was Black, and the other side of the street was White. So, the middle of the street was the dividing line.

I remember when we lived on Carnegie Street, our backyard backed up to White folks' yards. So, directly behind us were White folks. They would talk to us, but we were always just called: "Shirley, Pearl, gal, Girl, uncle" or that kind of stuff.

We didn't like it. We resented it, but at the same time we were not brave enough to speak out because you weren't willing to face the consequences. We would always have to address them as Mr. or Miss. When a White boy turned twelve, he was called Mister. He was no longer "Jim."

Black and White children did play together during this time. If you were a male Black no matter what your age was, the White people would refer to you as "boy" or whatever. However, the White children would be referred to as "Mr. or Miss." It was something else. And you always had to say: "Yes ma'am or No ma'am." We resented that but it was a part of the system that we were living in. That part was not good, but we learned how to survive in it. There were Colored and White drinking fountains and Colored and White entrances marked on the buildings in some of the places in Lauderdale Sub and all around Memphis.

Despite all of that within our neighborhood everybody just cared for each other. Everybody knew each other and looked out for each other. The adults, the neighbors, they looked out for everybody's children in the area. They'd say: "That's so and so's child." They'd tell you in a minute if they thought you were doing something wrong. "You stop and you better

CHAPTER 13: THE WESTBROOKS FAMILY

stop it now. I'm gonna tell your mama." And they were gonna tell her whether you stopped it or not.

When Alphonso finished high school he went to Talladega in Talladega, Alabama for two years and then he transferred to Lincoln University in Jefferson City, Missouri.

An example of the great achievers that came out of our family from the Lauderdale subdivision would be the fact that five of us Westbrooks ended up going to college and doing well as teachers and music directors. Some of us ended up with master's degrees and Logan received an honorary doctorate from LeMoyne-Owen College in 2014.

Al Jr., my oldest brother, moved to Chicago after college and he became the Communications Officer for Edison, the utility company in Chicago. My brother Logan became a record executive, and then he went on to own Source Records. Logan also eventually became the executive secretary of the Metropolitan Ecclesiastical Jurisdiction of Southern California and administrative assistant to the jurisdictional bishop. The three girls were teachers and coordinators in the Memphis City School system.

Pearl, Alphonso Jr., Shirley, Logan and Gloria Westbrooks

Cheryl Golden, PhD, Robert Lipscomb, MBA & Chairman of the Board of Trustees, Johnny B. Watson, President of LeMoyne-Owen, L.L.D, Jeff Johnson, Honorary Doctorate Recipient and Commencement Speaker 2014; Dr. Logan H. Westbrooks, Honorary Doctorate Recipient 2014.

On Carnegie Street and there was a family called the Moores. Peter Moore, Humphrey Moore Jr. and some of the other Moores. I don't remember all of their names, but I do remember Peter. He went on to Tennessee State University and he became a pilot for American Airlines until he retired. He's passed away now but he did that for fifteen to twenty years.

And then there were the Browns who lived on that street. I remember Garnett Brown, they called him "Tut." He had red hair and I believe he played with The Jazz Crusaders, Lionel Hampton, and Herbie Hancock. He did very well for himself. I remember we went to New York to see him. He always had first chair in whatever instrument that he played. His main instrument was the trombone. The Browns had two sisters and I know that Jean became a teacher, and the other one was Margaret

CHAPTER 13: THE WESTBROOKS FAMILY

Ann. She became a dental hygienist. She went on to Meharry Medical College (in Nashville).

Going on to the next block on Carnegie there was the Dandridge family. The Dandridge's did okay and going on further up were the Hawkins, they did alright. I remember there was one named Marylou (Mary Louise Hawkins Johnson Haile) and she moved on to D.C. and became an educator. Two of her sisters were also teachers. Ritta taught at Orleans Elementary and Claudia Hawkins taught at Hamilton Elementary. Another sister (Florence Hawkins) played the piano.

The only ones I can remember from Lauderdale Street would be the Bishops. Mrs. Bishop was a teacher, and she had a son. I remember we called him Jimmy Joe, but his name was James Bishop. He went on to M. I. T. (Massachusetts Institute of Technology) and he became some kind of scientist. I don't know what kind, but everybody was proud of him. Don't let me forget the Neelys. The Neelys came off of Lauderdale Street. They opened Interstate Barbeque and Interstate Barbecue is known worldwide. James opened his first place in 1978. He and his siblings, along with his nephews continued to grow the business. So now, the Neely name is famous worldwide.

Now let's go over to Cameron Street. The Bryants lived on that street and they were also members of the Church God in Christ. They went to Carnegie COGIC. Donald Bryant is a blues singer and he's still performing. He has a number of records out. The Londons also lived on that street. Hezekiah London became a boxer. He was nationally known and is now deceased.

Let's go to Latham. I think there was one lady who lived on Latham Street, her name is Sister Anderson. I don't know her first name, but I remember that she was a member of Carnegie COGIC. Carnegie had some influential members during that time.

There were many people that were at church who were really influential in society. Sister Anderson was a teacher for the Memphis City Schools during that time, and her husband was a letter carrier. They were very well-respected people and members of the church. I remember that she had a son. He finished college and moved on to Detroit. I remember when he was in high school, he played the trumpet.

My brother, Al Jr. was interested in blowing the trumpet. After Mrs. Anderson's son finished high school, he was no longer interested in the trumpet, so she gave that trumpet to my brother. Of course, he played it for a while and then he passed it on down in the family. I believe that one of my nephew's has it now. We still have that trumpet in the family. That was on Latham Street.

Okay, well let me go the other way. The Bradford's lived on that street (Latham Street) also. All of them did well and went to college and so forth. Of course, there were the Moores. Elder Moore was a sanctified preacher. He had a son named Warren Moore and Warren is a doctor now. So, he did well.

Back to the other side, going towards Lincoln School, that first street is McMillan. There were the Davenports. Herbert Davenport Jr. is deceased now, but he became a minister, and he pastored a large church (Shiloh Baptist) here in Memphis before his passing. He had several sisters. Hattie Marie Davenport Martin became a nurse. There was Magnolia Davenport and Ann and I believe they were nurses also. We still love every one of them. That's all we talked about on McMillan was the Davenports.

Then we go on up McMillan Street and there are the Porter Smiths at 1671 McMillan. I know the Porters are also from the Hawkins Davenport family. It's a small, small world.

I'm going to go to Webb Street before I go to Orleans because Dr. Hodges came off of that street. He became a dentist. Then we go over to Orleans and that's where the Patterson's lived. Mr. G.E. Patterson (Gilbert Earl Patterson) became the presiding bishop and a famous recording artist in the Church of God in Christ.

There was also Bishop J. O. Patterson (James Oglethorpe Patterson Sr.). They were cousins in the same family. He didn't live in the Lauderdale Sub.

Geri and Logan Westbrooks, Bishop Samuel Smith and Mrs. Lee Ella Patterson Smith, sister of Gilbert Patterson

Gilbert grew up on Orleans Street, which is right across the street from Lincoln School until his family moved to Detroit. All of his older siblings who also went to Lincoln School, Le Ella, Barbara, Mary, and WA Jr.

G. E. Patterson presided from 2000 to 2007 as presiding bishop of COGIC and J. O. Patterson presided from 1968 to 1989. There were one or two others in between (Bishop L. H. Ford 1990 to 1995 and Bishop C. D. Owens 1995 to 2000).

Louis Ford from Chicago succeeded J. O. Patterson. He was my brother's pastor in Chicago. Louis Ford became the presiding bishop after J. O. Patterson's death. Bishop Charles Blake Sr. succeeded G. E. Patterson as presiding bishop from 2001 to 2021.

G. E. Patterson

*Bishop Charles Blake
Sr. Presiding Bishop
COGIC 2007–2021*

Our faith and church were the ties that bound us together. I knew the Davenports because their grandmother was a member of Carnegie Church also. She was a Davenport (Virginia Hawkins Davenport). They were sort of indirectly affiliated with the Church of God in Christ.

The Davenports would attend every now and then with their grandmother. She lived with them.

I just remember Mother Hawkins from 1658 Carnegie. Looks like from my memory that she could play the piano.

I know one of the twins did (referring to Florence Hawkins) but I believe the mother did too. I'm not sure of that. I'm trying to remember because I was a child then. I know that she was one of the church mothers on the Mother's Board. She was an attractive looking lady.

CHAPTER 13: THE WESTBROOKS FAMILY

Willie G. Hawkins, Bible in hand, likely coming home from church to 1658 Carnegie Street. Circa 1955

Regarding the twins, I could never tell them apart although they were not identical. But I still would not get the names right. They were Florence and Floretta Hawkins. I remember Florence the most, the one who played the piano.

There was also Claudia and Ritta. Ritta moved to Washington, D.C. and later came back to Memphis. If I remember it right and she married Reverend M. L. Porter who was her first husband from Freeport, Illinois.

Note: *Ritta and Reverend M. L. Porter had two boys Roderick and Reginald Porter. She worked at Metropolitan Church in Washington, DC. Where she may have been the church secretary. That's where she met her husband. Then they moved to Illinois. That didn't work out and then she moved back to Memphis, Tennessee. Years later, she married another man named Stanie Smith, Sr. and that's when she moved from 1658*

Carnegie Street to 1671 McMillan Street on the corner of McMillan and Person. She had another son, Stanie Smith, Jr. Her sons excelled in law, government and international communications and the Air Force.

Marylou Hawkins Johnson (Haile) Marqueline Jackson (Gardner), Claudia Hawkins, Jackie Ray Johnson and baby Stanie Robin Smith at 1658 Carnegie Street

Ritta kept her house very nicely. At one point, she painted it White and blue, and it stayed that way until she died in 2013. The family maintained the house for several years afterwards before selling it to a family friend.

Mary Louise became a schoolteacher and administrator in Washington, D. C. before returning to Memphis in 1977 for a short stint. Sue, another sister, moved to Washington, D. C. and became one of the first Black lieutenants in the D.C. Correctional System.

Claudia Hawkins never married and worked as a teacher until she retired due to health reasons. The thing about Claudia is that I didn't know her until she was in her later years because she was a teacher also. And one

CHAPTER 13: THE WESTBROOKS FAMILY

of her sisters, it must have been Ritta, who would always assist her. If I remember correctly, she lost her eyesight near the end, but her sister would always bring her out. She wouldn't let her stay at home. She would help her and guide her along wherever she wanted to go. I remember those two sisters and then I remember the twins. In fact, I remember all of them.

Walter Hawkins Jr. at a broadcast studio

There was Walter Jr. who was the only son that resided on Carnegie. It was a remarkable family. I know that Walter had a sense of humor. He went to the eighth grade with me. So, he would have been the same age as I am. We went to the sixth, seventh and eighth grade together. Those three years were at Lincoln School. He's on the picture, too. I guess. I haven't looked at that picture in so long but I know I still have it.

I know the Hawkins family because their mother brought her children to Carnegie Church, just like my grandmother brought us to church.

It's remarkable how far we've all come. The prayers of those saints really prevailed.

Alice Westbrooks shares memories of Alphonso Westbrooks Jr.

Alice Westbrooks & Alphonso Westbrooks Jr.

My husband and I met in Talladega, Alabama. He was born and raised in Memphis, Tennessee and I grew up in Miami and Arizona. We moved to Chicago, Illinois around 1956.

We were both graduates of Historically Black Colleges and Universities (HBCUs). I proudly attended Talladega College in Alabama and graduated in 1955. Alphonso is a proud graduate of Lincoln University in Jefferson City, Missouri. We married on the day of Alphonso's graduation. Afterwards Alphonso got a Chicago Defender Newspaper scholarship to the University of Chicago for graduate school.

CHAPTER 13: THE WESTBROOKS FAMILY

Alphonso graduated from the University of Chicago with a Master of Journalism and then he enlisted in the U.S. Army. We lived in Europe while Alphonso was in the army for three years and I taught American students on the base. While stationed in France we traveled extensively in Europe visiting Belgium, Germany, and Spain. We bought a car that was our passport for exciting adventures.

In Belgium I went to see the great Ella Fitzgerald in concert and in Barcelona, Spain we were welcomed into the homes of kind Spanish strangers. We ate dinner with their family and slept well overnight. We learned to cook escargot and other French foods, returning with a collection of wine.

After the army we returned to Chicago. I worked as an elementary school teacher and my husband was employed by Helene Curtis and Ebony Magazine in corporate America working in marketing and journalism.

Eventually he was hired at Commonwealth Edison, where he was one of the first Black employees who rose through the ranks in marketing, and community affairs. He eventually led their Corporate Affairs Department in Chicago.

We became entrepreneurs and launched a brand that was the precursor to a store like Pier 1 or World Market that sold imported home furnishings and household goods from around the world. The inventory included items from more than 300 countries and specialized in African Art. We wanted to celebrate African culture and elevate African American history through the store. Eventually *Sticks and Stones* operated two locations on the south side of Chicago. My home is filled with African Art acquired while we had the business. The business closed after our family grew and we welcomed three daughters in 1968, 1970, and 1973.

I continued my career as an elementary school teacher with the Chicago Board of Education and retired after more than forty years of service at various public schools on the South Side of Chicago. After retirement from Con Edison, Alphonso worked with Bishop Louis Henry Ford and the Church of God in Christ as the Public Affairs and Public Relations representative for Bishop Ford. Alphonso had grown up with Bishop Ford and the Westbrooks family was among the founding members of the Church in Memphis, Tennessee.

Bishop Ford was very politically connected in Chicago. Alphonso encouraged him to campaign for Arkansas Governor Bill Clinton when he ran for President 1992. He supported Bishop Ford's vision to use political relationships to grow the church in Chicago. We attended Clinton's inauguration in 1993. Alphonso passed away in 1996.

Our daughters are all college graduates, and I am a grandmother of three. My grandson Chaz is a graduate of Howard University. He lives and works in Indianapolis, Indiana. My grandson Ian is in graduate school at Johns Hopkins and lives and works in Boston. My youngest grandson Aiden is a freshman in high school in Chicago.

CHAPTER 13: THE WESTBROOKS FAMILY

Pearl Westbrooks Hines shares memories of Lauderdale Sub

Pearl Westbrooks Hines

I am the fourth born in the Westbrooks family. We moved to Lauderdale Sub when I was in the third grade. I went to Lincoln School and continued through the eighth grade there.

I was in whatever they had going on at the school back in that day. We went to school and some days we went home for lunch and some days we stayed at school and ate in the cafeteria or across the hall in the auditorium. The cafeteria wasn't big enough for all of the students to eat there all at once. I graduated from Lincoln School in 1952 as number one in my class.

My friends were the Davenports. Hattie and Herbert Jr. were in my class, and I graduated with them. I was also friends with Francis Thomas. We were friends at Lincoln and on into our years at Booker T. Washington High School. Then Francis and I went to LeMoyne-Owen College together.

When I was in the tenth grade, we moved over to Latham Street. I also sang and we had an ensemble of six people. Rev. Townes Earlene's wife taught music class. She was Townes then, but she later married Rev. Holmes, when she went to Beulah Baptist. She was Mrs. Townes when we went to Lincoln. We had two eighth grade classes that finished at Lincoln. Mrs. Townes had a class and Miss Diamond had a class. Mrs. Townes was the music teacher during that time. Miss Diamond was the equivalent of our home room teacher.

The classes got bigger, and they enlarged the school. The next few years after that they moved the junior high over to the south side but that was well after I had left.

As for my musical ability, I sang at church and at school. When I graduated from Booker T. Washington High School, I went to LeMoyne on a music scholarship.

We were members of the Temple Church of God in Christ up there on Lauderdale and Georgia Street. Carnegie COGIC was up the street from where we lived. We could walk there. I could remember being in the church over there too. I sang solos at both churches.

l graduated in 1956 from high school. A lot of people from Lauderdale Sub were in the same class from elementary school on up through high school. We've been together through all of those times. Professor Washburn was the principal at Lincoln School.

He was the principal there when I was a senior in college when I went back to do my student teaching. He was rather proud that one of his

CHAPTER 13: THE WESTBROOKS FAMILY

students came back. I did not go back to work there; I just did my student teaching there.

In my opinion, I thought I had a wonderful childhood growing up in the neighborhood. I still see a lot of people who grew up in the area. A lot of people from Lauderdale Sub are still around but a lot of them have gone home to glory. Overall, I think it was some good years. We didn't have any problems. We grew up and moved on. I was next to the last child born. I was down in the ranks, but everything was fine and I enjoyed living in Lauderdale Sub.

Lincoln Elementary School Pearl Westbrooks' 8th Grade graduation. Far Right: Professor Washburn, Principal

CHAPTER 14

REGINALD SMITH & THE FAMILY DAY CARE

Book by Reginald F. Smith Sr.

I've written a book on the experience of growing up as an African American in Memphis during the late '50s and early '60s. In Memphis, Jim Crow was very rampant. And this term "Lauderdale Sub" is about a sub microcosm of a snapshot of a serious entity.

CHAPTER 14: REGINALD SMITH & THE FAMILY DAY CARE

It's almost unheard of to talk about growing up in the timeframe which I grew up in and not introduce that.

Everything said "Colored" or "Whites Only." Bathrooms and water coolers were marked for "Whites" or "Colored." We had to go to the balcony to go to the movies, which is now The Orpheum Theater. When we went to the zoo, we had a Colored day. If we went to the Mid-South Fair when it came to town, we went on "Colored" day.

We had our own Cotton Makers Jubilee. The White people had theirs down at Jefferson Davis Park and ours was at Church Park. There would be people circling the place on wagons and barbecuing. When you're talking about the roots of Memphis, you're talking about me. You're talking about my family.

My grandfather was Alphonso Westbrooks Sr. His job was to coordinate all the newspapers to be thrown around in Memphis and surrounding areas as far as Covington, Tennessee. The main newspapers for our people were the *Memphis World*, the *Tri-State Defender* and *The Call*.

Again, you had to go back to the time frame that we were in. Little Black boys were not given jobs. You couldn't even go out of your neighborhood. So essentially, my grandfather employed a majority of African American boys who grew up to be principals and teachers, including the mayor Willie Herenton (first African American mayor Memphis elected 1991 and served five terms.). His first job was working for my grandfather selling newspapers.

You could sell papers for a nickel and keep two pennies or three pennies to give back to my grandfather. So unbeknownst to all of us, what he did was to create African American entrepreneurs and train us to be self-sufficient and to depend on ourselves. That's what he was instilling in us.

They lived in the LeMoyne Gardens housing projects and then the family from there to a place called Carnegie Street.

Mrs. Erma Westbrooks, Gloria, Pearl, and Al Jr. at their home in LeMoyne Gardens

Since then, every African American family member in my family has gone to college, they own properties, they own businesses, and they do things that are astronomical to the world.

We started a day care here in Memphis called Caring Hearts Day Care Center and it was really the culmination of my mom and my aunts' ideas. They are retired teachers. My wife is a businessperson who works with and manages some offices here in Memphis.

We got together and decided to make a day care center a reality. "Saying" and "doing" are two different things. We found that out later. We had to make sure that all of the codes were in order and that everybody was safe in the building that we chose. We had to have inspectors come out and sign off on everything, which ended up being a good thing.

We made friends with the inspectors. Essentially, the day care opened by the grace of God. With a lot of prayer, hard work, and determination, it

CHAPTER 14: REGINALD SMITH & THE FAMILY DAY CARE

turned out to be a very successful and lucrative business. Everybody put in everything that they had by giving 100% of their efforts. Sometimes we'd go without a paycheck to make sure that the lights stayed on and that the children were fed, and everybody was happy.

Our motto was "To make weaker children stronger." That motto remained for the entire time that we were there, approximately 16 or 18 years. Essentially, during that timeframe we tried to instill in children what a lot of people said could not be instilled in African American children. "They can't learn," was a common notion. I beg to differ, and I take the opposite position one hundred percent. They can learn what you teach them.

We spent time educating our children and teaching them about phonetics, grammar, and pronunciation. We taught them about the seven continents and African American history. We taught them about putting on their seat belts and going out in space and looking at some of the other planets or visiting the moon.

We took take time as a group to learn about African American history. The first open heart surgery was by Dr. Daniel Hale Williams. We have so many different facets of African American history, from the discovery of blood plasma by Dr. Charles Drew to many more historic contributions.

I'm not going to try to go through all of who's who in African American history, but we tried our best to link certain things to them, so that they would have an opportunity to know about themselves and to have self-esteem.

We always championed Christianity. We were a Christian-based day care center. So, we spent time going through the Bible, explaining verses, singing Bible songs and giving the children physical inspiration to make a difference in their lives. Our whole objective was to make stronger individuals out of them and we met that goal in a lot of ways.

Some of the kids that graduated from our day care were around long enough to come back and work for us. We hit a lot of different milestones throughout the course of the time that we were open. Uncle Logan Westbrooks played a part financially and in management. Uncle Joseph Bowen, who is now deceased, did the same. We had an array of other people that helped to make it a reality. Basically, Caring Hearts Day Care Center stood sixteen or eighteen years. Eventually, we made a decision to close the business. That's pretty much an overview.

So, you know, we know we don't sit around and toot our own horn, we thank God for allowing us to be conduits and to do the work that we do. The Westbrooks name is synonymous with high achievers. We've cultivated just about anybody you can think of from teachers to lawyers to doctors, and we've always been a refuge for those who are downtrodden, as well.

We put out over 2500 beds in the city for underprivileged kids. A lot of times we've done things that other people don't even know anything about such as supplying food and just trying to fill in the gap to do the best we could to help others that couldn't help ourselves. That's what I came from, and we all love each other.

A murder amidst a Black person was seldom heard of. Abuse between a husband and a wife or a male being abusive to a female was seldom heard of. There were just certain rules and regulations that you just did not cross. That's what they instilled in us as African American people. It's just something that I hope and pray that comes to us again, to love and respect one another, and to love and respect ourselves.

We made sure that we carried ourselves in a manner that was not just respected in man's eyes but was respected in God's eyes. You realize that but for the grace of God, there go I. We tried to persevere with that type of mentality the entire time.

CHAPTER 14: REGINALD SMITH & THE FAMILY DAY CARE

So first, the day care had to be put together. My aunts and my mother were teachers. When I grew up, I shined shoes, I emptied garbage cans, I worked in restaurants, I did busboy work and sold newspapers. I did whatever I could do, to make a living as an African American, young man. As long as it was legal and not immoral and not something that I could look back on and say there's some that I just wish I had never done. God blessed me to come through all of that and to be the man that I am now. I have raised two children. My son is in Chattanooga, he's married with two children and he's over the Bethlehem Center, which is a $3 million non-profit and one of the biggest non-profits in Chattanooga.

My daughter Regina, she's over the Southeast region of Walmart, which is about seven states. She's an engineer. She's worked at Kraft, Coca Cola, and Kellogg's and now she's at Walmart. She's over those stores and she makes sure the produce and everything runs correctly.

Both of them own real estate and are goal oriented. Hopefully God has allowed me to be able to teach them what I didn't have as a child. I met my father when I was 16. I say this to every young man when I teach them, that not having is not an excuse for not getting. You know what you want in life, somebody to teach you how to tie a tie, somebody to teach you how to get in line, how to get respect and be nice to women and one another. These are the things that I try to instill in children and teach them that just because you weren't there, you know what you want to have. Be that. If you do that, then you're doing what God sent you to do.

You're being a respectful man, you're being a good father, you're being a good husband and you're carrying a load that every African American man and woman has carried. Then, we have no problem. The problem we have is that we're not together.

The problem is not them, it's not the laws, it's not that. We're not together. When we are together, we can be happy and we can make a change.

More Memories of the Day Care Center from Shirley Westbrooks Smith

We ran it for almost twenty years. The day care was in Southeast Memphis on Knight Arnold Road. Our specialty was for children aged six weeks to five years. We also kept school aged children up to twelve years old before school and after school. Then we would transport them to their regular schools. During the summer, we would have a camp for those older students. It was operated by me, Pearl, and my son Reginald. We were the owners, actually we were three co-owners.

We had an infant caregiver. In fact at one time we had two. Then we had two-year-olds. We call them toddlers. We had two classes of those. Then there were the three-year-olds and the four and five-year-olds were together. So, we had about six teachers. And then we had a cookbook. We didn't have a house cleaner. We did our cleaning. We were a three-star center.

We opened it in the mid-'90s around 1994 or 1995, and we were in business until I think, 2012 or 2013. It was around twenty years.

The school was founded by two young ladies who at one time grew up or lived in the Lauderdale Sub and became educators. We were educated at Lincoln, and then Booker T. Washington. The education from those schools and our post-secondary education inspired us to create another educational institution outside of Lauderdale Sub.

We had retired, and we were a little bored. We didn't know what to do with ourselves. So, I got a job at the IRS. We had to be there at 8 o'clock in the morning and you had to have your ID. They had so many rules. I

CHAPTER 14: REGINALD SMITH & THE FAMILY DAY CARE

was hanging in there. I did it one or two seasons. Then I said, I am tired of this. I can't go by his regimentation. I said what can we do?

Actually, it was my son Reginald who came up with what we could do. At the time he had two children that were fairly young. So, we could do a day care center because we realized that a lot of people were looking for quality day care and we had the expertise to do it. So, let's try it.

We found a building and fixed it up to a day care center with classrooms, the kitchen, the bathrooms and all the things that the state required, and we opened a day care. We did real good with it, I got to say that. Some of our kids are mostly grown now. They have finished college. A lot of them have finished college. They would always say, I got off to a good start because of the foundation.

We had graduations. We had Christmas programs. We would have Santa and my son Reginald would dress in the Santa suit. We would get people from outside the day care center to come and take a picture with the Black Santa. Our kids were taught the basics. When they went to school they knew the basics. They could write their names, they knew their addresses, and they knew their ABC's.

There were two teachers who I really thought had a great influence on me growing up. The one I remember most was James Taylor. He was my seventh-grade teacher. I never did know what he majored in but evidently, he majored in English because he really could teach English. He instilled in us the parts of speech. I know the parts of speech to this day.

Or course my mother and father instilled in us a zeal for learning. Keep in mind, I went to kindergarten at the age of three. All of us started school at age three. I think the tuition was a quarter a week. That amounted to about a nickel per child. People would ask how Mr. Westbrooks could afford to send his children to school. The secret was that he knew the importance of education.

CHAPTER 15

REFLECTIONS FROM LOGAN H. WESTBROOKS

Memories of the Lauderdale Sub, Education, Aspirations, Hard Work, The Music Industry and beyond.

After reading and hearing so much about the condition, not only of Memphis, but of Lauderdale Sub in particular, I decided to share my formative years and roots with my two nephews, Alfred Michael Moore and Reginald Smith.

I also decided that maybe I should formulate my thoughts in book form. So that was the beginning of this project.

Lauderdale Sub is considered one of the most depressed neighborhoods in the city of Memphis at the time of publication and has been for a number of years. Memphis sits alongside the Mississippi River, making it a prime transit town for shipping and railways. Today, the city is home to the global transport giant FedEx and Memphis is the 2nd largest cargo airport next to Hong Kong, according to Airports Council International.

Elon Musk has selected Memphis as the home of xAI, a "Gigafactory of Compute" site. Basically, it's the world's largest supercomputer.

CHAPTER 15: REFLECTIONS FROM LOGAN H. WESTBROOKS

Although South Memphis has historically tracked disproportionately low numbers for public health, education, and poverty by many statisticians, ironically at one time it was also home to many government officials, business owners, educators, faith leaders, entertainers and other decorated and celebrated national personalities.

I am definitely a product of Lauderdale Sub. There were some really great things that came out of the Lauderdale Sub. Against unbelievable odds, many successful people attained great achievements.

Cousins: Rear: Horace and Rose Bowen, Shirley and Pearl Westbrooks. Front: Erma Jean Bowen and Alma Jones

The Lauderdale Sub, as I remember from my childhood memories, existed during the heavily segregated area of Memphis, Tennessee. It's primarily an all-Black neighborhood.

My family lived at 1500 Carnegie Street, and there were actually some White folks that lived directly behind us, which was within those parameters. It was sort of short lived because there are many who eventually moved away. So spottily, there were a few White families that were still scattered around in primarily the Black area, but eventually they all disappeared as well.

So, it became just about 100% Black. Lauderdale Sub would also be known as the area that Lincoln Elementary School serviced, as Lincoln Elementary School is located on Orleans Street. That would comprise the boundaries of Lauderdale Sub as I envisioned. There's a time limit too. I'm thinking in terms of around 1945 up until about 1961 or 1962.

1500 Carnegie Address Plate

Logan Westbrooks 10, Pearl 9, Gloria 2, July 4, 1947

CHAPTER 15: REFLECTIONS FROM LOGAN H. WESTBROOKS

There were other areas in Memphis as well. There was the Klondike area, there was Orange Mound, which was primarily an all-Black area and incidentally, it was one of the oldest areas in Memphis in terms of Black folks buying homes. North Memphis was also a Black area.

There was also an area called Hollywood, which was a Black area. My experiences in Lauderdale Sub involved my interaction with the neighbors, my playmates, and other families in Lauderdale Sub.

My maternal grandmother was Mary Scruggs Bowen. She was born in 1884, just nineteen years after slavery ended. She married Horace, and they had fourteen children, one of which was my mother Erma Bowen Westbrooks.

Left: Mary Scruggs Bowen, holding her youngest child Joseph.
Right: Horace Bowen, grandfather and Callie Mae Bowen Lynch, aunt of Logan Westbrooks

Mary and her cousin Callie Tony got saved at a tent revival led by Elder Foster. He later became pastor of the Texas Street Mission. My grandmother's home caught fire on Texas Street and then she moved to a home on College Street.

Soon after she joined the saints at the Carnegie Church of God in Christ. She remained a member until her death in 1951.

My mother was primarily at home raising the children. My father was the circulation manager of the *Memphis World* newspaper. Of course, he always also had a second job, which was at the *Commercial Appeal* newspaper.

Young Henry Westbrooks (brother of Logan's father), Alphonso Westbrooks Sr. (in the car), and Joseph Bowen (brother of Erma Bowen Westbrooks).

That newspaper was printed at night, and he was one of the people responsible for driving the truck that would drop newspapers in bulk quantities throughout the city. It was the morning paper. Those are the two jobs that he had. He worked for the *Memphis World* newspaper in the daytime. Then at night, he would go to work around eight or nine

CHAPTER 15: REFLECTIONS FROM LOGAN H. WESTBROOKS

in the evening at the *Commercial Appeal*. I think he worked there until about maybe about five or six in the morning.

When we lived in LeMoyne Garden we were fortunate. We had one of the largest apartments that was available in the project. LeMoyne Gardens was a government subsidized project, and we had a three-bedroom apartment. If I'm not mistaken, the actual rent that my parents were paying went up about 10 to 15 cents monthly. Then my father decided to buy a house. He could buy a house cheaper than what he was paying in rent in LeMoyne Gardens.

So, he found a house in Lauderdale Sub at 1500 Carnegie Street. He saw the potential of expanding because we moved from a three-bedroom apartment with five children. He added two bedrooms, a walk-in closet, a side porch, and a door that led from the kitchen to the outside. The house also had a shed in the rear that my brother converted into his office. My father also had the bathroom enclosed on the back porch. There was now a bedroom for my brother and me, and a bedroom for my two sisters. Then of course my young sister Gloria was just a toddler. She slept in the room there with my parents in the third bedroom.

My family was constantly making the best of what they had. I can't pinpoint what exact effect that had on me, but for sure my father was the circulation manager for the largest Black-owned newspaper in the city. Early on I was influenced by a man who commanded his territory.

It also meant that I always had a job selling newspapers, whether it was selling them door to door with a set route, of it there were certain kinds of major annual events going on in the city, like the National Baptist Convocation, a 21-day international convention for the Church of God in Christ. This takes place even now. The *Memphis World* newspaper had headlines, stories and pictures about the National Baptist Convention that took place at Ellis auditorium in Memphis one year.

As a kid, I sold newspapers to all the delegates at the convention. It was held at East Georgia Avenue and Lauderdale Street, which was the mother church, the church that was pastored by Bishop C. H. Mason.

I also had my regular route and my regular customers that I'd be servicing with the newspaper. So, I always had a job I would say from about third grade on.

The newspapers sold for about seven cents, and I think I got about two cents off every newspaper. That's why I always had a pocket full of money.

The Mother Church at 672 S. Lauderdale that I knew as a child was also the site of the Holy Convocation prior to the completion of Mason Temple

The Mother Church at 672 S. Lauderdale that I knew as a child was also the site of the Holy Convocation prior to the completion of Mason Temple

The Church of God in Christ (founded by Charles Harrison Mason) was located at 672 South Lauderdale. He was pastor of that church and traveled all over the country launching new churches and new jurisdictions. The church at Georgia and Lauderdale is called the Temple and is known as the Mother Church.

CHAPTER 15: REFLECTIONS FROM LOGAN H. WESTBROOKS

It was a time of dedication, fasting and praying. He would have people from all over the country that were members of the Church of Christ. Then of course, things are segregated in Memphis.

So, you had delegates that were staying in people's houses. They'd pay them a certain amount of money for the entire time that they were in Memphis. Initially the convocation would last about three weeks. They have since cut it down to less than a week, but initially it lasted for three weeks. It could have been as much as 21 days back then.

Mrs. Erma Bowen Westbrooks

I can remember my mother taking us on trips looking at other houses, not only in Lauderdale Sub but in other areas as well. I'm 90% sure that she was the one that found that house and we eventually moved in on Latham Street. She took the lead in that. She was constantly looking for a better way, better accommodations, a nicer neighborhood, a nice front yard, a nice backyard, and better schools for her children.

My mother came from a very humble background. It wasn't that she came from a fabulous, wealthy, middle class family. That wasn't the case. She just had aspirations for her children. It was always to make things better for her children. They had to be educated to do better and go further. That was instilled in me from her, more so than from my father.

My high school years were spent on Latham Street. When I finished high school, I enrolled at LeMoyne-Owen College, which was on Walker Street. Consequently, I can remember walking from LeMoyne-Owen College all the way down Walker Street to our home on Latham Street.

Booker T. Washington Class 10-5A Miss P. S. Bolden Front row, 3rd from the left is Logan Westbrooks.

Blair T. Hunt Jr. (1888–1978) Educator, civic and religious leader, was the son of former slaves. He was educated at LeMoyne and Morehouse Colleges, Roger Williams and Tennessee State A & I. He was the principal of Booker T.

CHAPTER 15: REFLECTIONS FROM LOGAN H. WESTBROOKS

Washington High School from 1932-1959. He was the first pastor of Mississippi Boulevard Christian Church.
Source: HMdb.org (Historical Marker Database)

I secured an Improved Benevolent Protective Order of Elks of the World (IBPOEW) scholarship and was recommended by Blair Hunt, the principal of Booker T. Washington High School.

The Improved Benevolent Protective Order of Elks of the World (IBPOEW) scholarship was granted for $1,000.00.

Logan Westbrooks

I spent two years at LeMoyne-Owen College. My brother attended Talladega College on a scholarship in Talladega, Alabama. He attended for two years at Talladega and then he transferred to Lincoln University in Jefferson City, Missouri. He wanted to become a journalist, which is what he eventually became. They had a school of journalism at Lincoln University, and he was able to secure an Abbott scholarship. It was named after Robert S. Abbott, the founder of *The Chicago Defender* newspaper in 1905.

My brother graduated from Lincoln University with a degree in journalism and that's what eventually turned me on to Lincoln University. I transferred to Lincoln University and spent the next two years in Jefferson City, Missouri where I majored in business administration.

I graduated in 1955 from Booker T. Washington High School, then two years at LeMoyne and spent three years at Lincoln University. I think it was 1960 or 1961 when I left Lincoln University. There at Booker T. Washington High School I continued to sell newspapers. I had teachers who were my customers. So, I think the *Memphis World* newspaper would be dropped off every Thursday at school and I would sell newspapers to the faculty as well as to some of the students. That was my job during the day at school. Of course, I still had my regular newspaper route.

Then my classmate Moses Thomas was working in the kitchen at Methodist Hospital. On Moses referral, I was hired at Methodist during my third and fourth year in high school. Then, a cousin of ours owned a restaurant called Tony's Inn. It was one of the most exclusive steak houses for Colored people at the time. My stint at Methodist Hospital taught me about food prep, cooking and setting up banquets. I also befriended the head chef and worked banquets for the doctors and nurses. I helped prepare and serve the food.

Next, I started working at Tony's Inn as a waiter. Consequently, the two years when I was at LeMoyne, I was also working at Tony's Inn at night as a waiter and on weekends. When I enrolled at Lincoln University in Jefferson City, I would come home in the summer and work at Tony's Inn to make what I needed for school expenses.

CHAPTER 15: REFLECTIONS FROM LOGAN H. WESTBROOKS

Even there in Jefferson City, Missouri I had several jobs. My main job was as a representative for RJ Reynolds Tobacco Company. They were based in Winston Salem, North Carolina. I was a student representative. This is a job where tobacco companies would hire students to work on various college campuses and pass out sample cigarettes. It provided a great income. They produced several tobacco products, and I passed out Camel cigarettes, Winston cigarettes and menthol cigarettes. That was my job.

I had now mastered the art of waiting tables and I was honing my skills in marketing as a student employee at RJ Reynolds. My many skills and jobs gave me additional income. While at Lincoln University I was able to buy a car.

On weekends, I would load up several guys from Memphis and I would charge them a certain amount of money and drive them to Memphis. This would give some of them an opportunity to go home over the weekends. So that was also additional income.

Then there was another job that I created. I saw that there was a shortage of student housing for freshmen men on campus. There were about half a dozen huge two-story houses where some of the affluent Black doctors and lawyers had lived near the campus. Their houses were not exactly abandoned, but they moved further away into the suburbs. So, those houses were just there. Consequently, I approached several of them and I was able to rent those houses and convert them into student housing.

The university had a number of surplus beds that they had stored in the veterans' barracks, because right after World War II or right after the Korean conflict, they had an influx of veterans that were going to college. They were called the veterans barracks. Those beds were no longer in use.

I got the school to lend me those beds and dressers and other such necessities. I rented three houses and I put male freshman students in those houses, and that brought me additional income. I was doing all sorts of things in terms of making money and that was until I graduated.

I was drafted into the service, and I spent twenty-four months in the army. I was drafted out of Memphis, Tennessee for twenty-four months. After basic training in Arkansas, I was transferred to Fort Bragg North Carolina. I guess I had about twenty to twenty-one months left to serve. While there at Fort Bragg, North Carolina, I went to the Non-Commissioned Officer's Club, which was the largest club on the base. I got a job there as a waiter.

Because of my experience and expertise, I eventually became the head waiter there. I was really running the entire club. I did that until my time was up and I got out, came back through Memphis, and made my way to Chicago. I really wanted to be there because my brother was living in Chicago.

So, I went to the Urban League where I learned of an opening at Johnson Publishing Company for a merchandising salesman. I met with John Johnson, the publisher of Ebony and Jet Magazine. I was hired for that position. The merchandising department was based in New York City. Mr. Johnson sent me to New York City for a couple of weeks of training at the offices there.

I returned to Chicago and was based there out of the home office. I did that for about a year. Then the Urban League notified me of a position that RCA Victor was trying to fill.

The RCA Corporation was particularly interested in recruiting Black men for management training positions. They had a position that was available in Chicago, and they also had a position that was available in Detroit, Michigan.

In Detroit they hired Tom Draper. I was hired in Chicago and entered the training program. Tom entered in Detroit. We both started in the

CHAPTER 15: REFLECTIONS FROM LOGAN H. WESTBROOKS

management training program and worked in various areas of the company to figure out which was the best fit. Are you better in territory sales, are you better in records or in some other areas? The training program helped determine the best course for their new hires.

At that particular time, RCA Victor was distributing the Whirlpool washers and dryers. They were selling them out of the offices there in Des Plaines, Illinois. They also had what was called a home entertainment center. A huge Black and White television set had a record player and a radio combined and built into the design. They called it a home in home entertainment center. These were sold and distributed out of the Des Plaines facility.

RCA was also distributing records out of that same facility. This included all of the recordings that were on RCA Victor, including Elvis Presley's records. One day there was an RCA recording artist that was coming to town to one of the major hotels located downtown. It was going to be a dinner show. I recently got married and I saw this as an opportunity to treat my wife to a nice dinner and a show. I think it was a country and western act, that was appearing. I wasn't really into country and western music but I liked the idea of going to a show at this fabulous hotel, and having dinner at the company's expense as a newlywed.

I asked the sales manager in the record department about an invitation to go to that show.

He said: 'Are you interested in records as a Record Rep?'

I said: 'Yes!'

Naturally, I was interested because if I worked in the record division, I could attend events like this. It didn't matter that I didn't have a clue what a record rep did but for my next assignment, I was transferred over to the record division. I trained in that division as a backup to the sales staff. I would go into major retail stores and do inventory as I was learning the business.

As an example, "Rose Record" store was one of the largest record stores in the country. They had huge inventories of every artist on the RCA label. They had a minimum of five copies of everything in the catalog. I would go through the inventory, and if the inventory calls for five units and there's only two in stock, this means that three had been sold and I needed to place an order to bring the inventory back up to what it should be. I recorded my findings on a small tape recorder and then transcribed it, critiqued it, and turned it over to the salesperson that was servicing that particular outlet. They in turn would prepare the order to replace what should be there.

As I was learning this part of the retail record business, the 8-track tape entered the marketplace. It was completely new. None of the sales staff wanted to be bothered. At the beginning, the 8-track tape player was sold through service stations. The reason being was that the Learjet 8-track tape player would be sold and installed in a service station.

They prepared a rack that held a certain number of 8-track tapes. A person could come in to have an 8-track tape machine installed in their car and then select 8-track tapes to purchase for the newly installed machine for their car.

So, I started opening up outlets and service stations throughout the Chicago area to sell and install 8-track tapes. As I moved around and met other salesmen, I became aware of a position for a territory salesman at Capitol Records. They wanted to hire their first Black salesman, so I applied for the position and was hired.

As their first and only Black salesman, naturally, I was given all of the Black accounts. There weren't that many at the time. By the same token, I had to put together a complete territory. I had a lot of White accounts as well. I also had a lot of classical, country, and western accounts.

CHAPTER 15: REFLECTIONS FROM LOGAN H. WESTBROOKS

Additionally, I had accounts that were on the far Westside, which were all White, and I had some accounts down in Southern Illinois, which accounted for a lot of overnight trips.

As a territory salesman at Capitol Records, I became aware of an opening for a job as a promotion representative or a Promo rep, as it is often called. This is the person who goes into a radio station to persuade the program director to play the records that you're bringing in on your label.

I became aware of an open position as a territory promotion rep for the Midwest. This job was based in Chicago. It included Detroit, Michigan and all of the Midwest, Cleveland, Cincinnati, Pittsburgh, Louisville, Kentucky, St. Louis, Missouri and Kansas City, Missouri. That was my territory. I would go in and service all of the radio stations in those cities. I did that for about a year.

An executive named Reggie Lavong was hired as the national promotion manager at Capitol. He was the program director for WWRL in New York City. Capitol Records hired him as a national promotion manager based in Hollywood. At this time Holland Dozier Holland (the Motown songwriting team) were in the process of finalizing their deal with Capitol Records as a distributor of their products. I spent about three or four days in Detroit with Reggie Lavong while he was there at Holland Dozier Holland's office as we were working out the structuring of that deal.

Then I went back to my regular job in Chicago. When Reggie went back to his home office in California he asked if I would like to come to California as his administrative assistant. Of course, this promotion came with more money and an opportunity to move to California. I said, "Of course, absolutely."

We worked out the deal and I was transferred to Los Angeles, California to work in Hollywood in the Capitol tower as the administrative assistant to the Vice President of Marketing.

I was in that position for less than a year. Then I became aware of a position in Chicago, Illinois at Mercury Records. I'm the assistant to the VP of Marketing and Promotions for Capitol Records, but now here is a position that is open where I would be the head of the department.

I interviewed with Mercury Records and met with President Irv Steinberg and his assistant, and I was hired for that position. Some of the artists on the label were Jerry Butler, Gene Chandler, Melba Moore, Buddy Miles, Rod Stewart, Erroll Garner and many more. The Mercury Records roster was vast.

I accepted that position, and I was in Mercury for less than a year. That's when I got the call from Clive Davis and Bruce Lundvall in New York. I met with them, and they were in the process of creating a Black music division and asked me to be the head of the department. That's when I went to work for CBS Domestic.

To date I have worked at RCA, Capitol, Mercury, and CBS. I had just started working for CBS in New York, CBS International. Then it was on to Soul Train Records and eventually my own label, Source Records in 1978.

Logan Westbrooks

CHAPTER 16

CARNEGIE CHURCH OF GOD IN CHRIST

Memories from Mother Dorothy McNeal, wife of the late Samuel Evans McNeal Jr.

Carnegie Church of God in Christ, now known as Gloryland Deliverance Temple COGIC

In the beginning, I was not here. I came in 1972, the year that my husband and I moved back from Chicago. I'm originally from Memphis, but I was a child when my dad moved up north. So, after getting married to Samuel McNeal and moving back here, that's when I became a member here. My father-in-law Elder RC McNeal was the pastor.

Elder R. C. McNeal
1889–1985

Elder Samuel E. McNeal
Sr. 1934–2020

At the time it was Carnegie Church of God in Christ, but now it is Gloryland Deliverance Temple. And the thing was, we were a very vibrant church. A lot of the saints now, the Lord has taken them on. It was very vibrant, and we had a lot of young people.

We had monthly meetings here. We had Tuesday night service, Friday night service and Sunday service. There were services on Sunday during the day, in the afternoon at 6:00 pm, which was Young People Willing Workers (YPWW).

When thinking of the legacy of faith, my son continued the work of his father, and my son Stephen has taken it from there.

The prayers prayed by the elders of the neighborhood, Mother Hawkins, Mother Wesson, Mother Holman, Mother Anderson, Mother Green

CHAPTER 16: CARNEGIE CHURCH OF GOD IN CHRIST

come to mind. Those are some of the older saints. They were all active mothers in the church. Also, there was Mother Arthur, and she lived several streets over. They were all active mothers.

Tuesday mornings we had prayer from 10:00 am until 11:00 am. A lot of them have gone on to glory and they were very faithful. Some have moved out of the state, but others are yet here. Mother Fannie Dukes is here, and she lives a few streets over. Her sister (Sister Moore) was very faithful. She left us just a few months ago. Mother Fannie Mae Dukes is the oldest member that is here now. These other members have come on in the latter years.

There have been so many things that have been done through the prayers of the saints and the leaders and the way that the people have lived for the Lord. They have given their life to the Lord and He has brought them through sicknesses and conditions. We have one right now that the Lord has just lifted her off of her bed having cancer, and she is here today.

Others have had the Lord bless them to get off walkers and things of that nature. That was through the prayers of the saints and through their living for God, doing what God wanted them to do. The Lord brought me through a surgery that I had on the 31st of January 2024. I had one of my aortic valves replaced, and I am up and about. It was nobody but God. I'm here because evidently, my work has not been completed and I thank God.

I want the world to know that the Lord is blessing Gloryland Deliverance Temple (formerly Carnegie Church of God in Christ). The pastors have been faithful to God and taken care of the leaders and the membership and they are teaching the people how to live for the Lord.

The original pastor of Carnegie Church of God in Christ was Elder RC McNeal from 1926 until his passing in 1985. He was succeeded by his son Elder Samuel E. McNeal until his passing in 2020. He was succeeded by his son Pastor Stephen C. McNeal.

Mother Dorothy McNeal and son, Stephen McNeal, current pastor of Gloryland Deliverance Temple.

LaRita Shelby (Lauderdale Sub book project manager) granddaughter of Willie G. Hawkins, who attended Carnegie COGIC, Missionary Barbara Coleman, Mother Dorothy McNeal, and Missionary & First Lady Sharyece McNeal.

CHAPTER 17

MORNING VIEW BAPTIST CHURCH

Addie Arnice Davenport Matthews recalls a lifelong membership at Morning View Baptist Church

Photo Courtesy of Magnolia Matthews, Circa 1960s

As I remember, I was baptized at twelve years old. That's when all of the kids in the family got baptized. Our father (Herbert Davenport Sr.) was a member of Morning View, and our mother (Addie Westbrook Davenport) was a member of a Methodist Church. So, she sent us to church at Morning View.

I was born in 1942, so I was twelve in 1954. I don't remember the founder of church, but we have all of their pictures on the wall now. I do recall Rev. John Johnson, and I think it was Rev. John L. Reynolds after that and then it was Rev. Wortham.

Rev. L. D. Saunders 1924–1934

Rev. John Johnson 1934–1956

Rev. John L. Reynolds 1956–1965

Rev. Lewis D. Wortham 1965–2005

CHAPTER 17: MORNING VIEW BAPTIST CHURCH

Rev. Alvin Fleming 2005–2022   *Rev. Ronald Claxton 2023*

When we went to church and stayed at church all day. We went to Sunday School, then we went to church service, then we went to Baptist Young People's Union (BYPU). This taught young Christian discipleship. That was just on Sunday.

Then in the summertime, we went to Vacation Bible School, and we also had the annual picnic down at Fuller Park. It used to be held at one of the city's designated Black parks at the time, Lincoln Park on Bellevue Blvd. This is not to be mistaken for the park adjacent to Lincoln School. Bellevue Blvd was later named Elvis Presley Blvd.

Back then Vacation Bible School used to last a whole a week but now it lasts for three or four days. Rev. Johnson was the pastor during my childhood. He baptized all of my sisters and brothers. The church also helped the poor. They bought things for the children in the neighborhood in those days. Mr. Bishop initiated that part of the church's missionary work in the community. If anybody needed anything, he made sure that they had it. I remember a lot of the older members such as Miss Pulliam and all those different people.

Morning View continues to be a thriving church. I think that is because it was the largest church in the neighborhood, and it had large families there. It was the Davenports, the Matthews, the Brandons, the Mitchells, the Haleys, and all of these people had children and grandchildren. They just never stopped growing. That's what I think. Everybody had six, seven or eight children and so that made it continue to grow. Currently, I go to my late brother's church (Shiloh Baptist, former pastor Rev. Herbert Davenport Jr.) but even now, a lot of the family members are still coming back to Morning View.

Since I've been there the church has not experienced a split. We've never had a dispute with our pastors. Rev. Johnson was there for a long time. Everybody loved him, as well as Rev. Wortham. It is rumored that a church spilt happened many years prior and that's how Mt. Sinai was formed.

The best part of Morning View being in the neighborhood is that we have the same families from way back. The church is now comprised of the children, and the children's children. They are still there. A lot of left, but they have come back. This is why we have been able to sustain and expand.

The neighborhood would not be the same without Morning View. A lot of families no longer live in the area, but they still come to Morning View.

Morning View Baptist Church is located at 1626 Carnegie Street, Memphis, Tennessee 38106. The current pastor is Rev. Ronald Claxton.

CHAPTER 18

MT. SINAI MISSIONARY BAPTIST CHURCH

Memories from Mary Ann Borders Mitchell

Mary Ann Borders Mitchell

Mt. Sinai Missionary Baptist Church is located at 1667 South Lauderdale Street. It has also been a long-standing house of worship in Lauderdale Sub.

I will start with when my mother first came to Memphis. Her first name is Rosie. Lee is her middle name, so it's not together. It's Rosie Lee Borders. My mother and father arrived in Memphis in 1947. My father's name was Benny.

They came to Memphis from Shelby, Mississippi and they immediately joined Mt. Sinai Missionary Baptist Church.

They joined in 1947 and the pastor in 1947 was Rev. L. L. Laws. Rev. M. J. Jenkins preceded him but I don't remember him. I was born in 1948. I have lived at our home at 1661 Carnegie Street since then.

Rev. M. J. Jenkins & Rev. L. L. Laws

What I remember about Mt. Sinai is that we went to church every Sunday when we were growing up. As the years went on my mother became the Sunday School superintendent. She also presided over the children's Easter program. She worked on the Mother's Board, and it was extra special when we celebrated Mother's Day at church. My mother also was over the Sunday school picnic. She did quite a few things as a lifetime member there. My dad worked in the church too. He was one of

CHAPTER 18: MT. SINAI MISSIONARY BAPTIST CHURCH

the trustee deacons. They made the decisions for the church and all that kind of stuff. He worked at the church until he passed away.

As a child I sang in the choir until I came of age. When my children Angela and Ricky were born, they also sang in the little children's choir. So, after that we just grew up and then we separated from that church. We had a lot of fun there.

The church picnic was at Fuller Park. When we went on our picnic the kids from the other churches would go along with us. They would rent a school bus.

I do remember Mother Hawkins from 1658 Carnegie. She would take me, Marq, Rod and Dank on what they called an "Around the World" trip. That was actually a day when we'd get on a bus and go to different people's houses.

Each house had prepared food from a different part of the country or the world. I might have Hawaiian food at my house and then we'd go to another person's house and they might have spaghetti and whatever else they have on the table for you to eat. At the end of the trip, you would have had a full dinner.

Also, when we were kids, Miss Ritta (Hawkins Porter) and Dank (Reginald Porter Sr.) gave me a birthday party. I'm not sure how old we were but Miss Ritta wrote an article about our party and put it in the Tri-State Defender newspaper. I'll never forget that.

Currently, I still live in my childhood home in Lauderdale Sub. It is one of the few homes still standing and in great condition. Of all of my childhood memories, I'd say the best part was Christmas. I remember my mother in the kitchen and the smell of the turkey and the dressing and all that she was cooking.

Another beloved memory is of Vacation Bible School at Mt. Sinai. My mother was over Vacation Bible School too. Those elders back then taught what they knew to teach, and they taught us well.

Here are the other pastors of Mt. Sinai in Lauderdale Sub.

Rev. R. L. Leaks Sr.

Rev. Henry Jackson 2000–Present

CHAPTER 19

REFLECTIONS

A Life of Service and Legacy

Logan & Geri Westbrooks

As I reflect on the journey of my life, I am filled with a deep sense of gratitude and purpose. My path has been one of unwavering service to others, shaped by the values instilled in me from an early age. My mother taught me to always share and be thankful and these lessons resonated throughout my life.

These teachings were reinforced by the role that my church, Carnegie COGIC, and The Temple played in my upbringing. I fondly remember the guidance of Father Christmas and Brother Mayfield at The Temple, whose wisdom shaped my understanding of faith, community, and service.

Throughout my years of schooling, I encountered countless mentors whose influence would stay with me forever. My sixth-grade teacher, Mrs. Gladys Broadnax, my high school principal Blair T. Hunt and Rev. James A. McDaniel of Bethel Presbyterian Church were among the pivotal figures in my life. Rev. McDaniel was a radio host on WDIA, and I was invited on his show numerous times. Mrs. McClellan, my ninth grade homeroom teacher, Mrs. Anna Hubbard Roberts, my twelfth-grade advisor, also helped me believe in the power of education and personal responsibility.

From the early days as a paperboy, I learned the importance of self-sufficiency and perseverance. Throughout my youth, I paid for my way through college after receiving a $1,000 scholarship from the Improved Benevolent Protective Order of Elks of the World (IBPOEW), upon the recommendation of my high school principal Blair T. Hunt.

Every job I took from shining shoes to waiting tables to selling newspapers, taught me invaluable lessons in hard work, responsibility, and people skills. Being a paperboy in Memphis also allowed me to engage with local doctors and lawyers on Beale Street, such as Dr. Watson and lawyers Benjamin Hooks and James Estes. These interactions were formative, teaching me the power of professional relationships and the impact of community leaders.

CHAPTER 19: REFLECTIONS

My parents were constant sources of encouragement. Their support, along with that of my siblings, created a strong and loving foundation.

Alphonso Westbrooks Sr. receives 25 years of service acknowledgement from the Memphis Publishing Company. March 28, 1971

Together, we worked as a close-knit family, bound by love, faith, and determination, which provided me with the strength to excel in all my endeavors.

In high school, my role as a student leader set the stage for my future activism. At LeMoyne-Owen College, I had the privilege of attending a film presentation about Martin Luther King Jr. and the Montgomery bus boycott. This sparked something deep within me, alongside my friends Marion Barry, Kenneth Cole, and Allen Hammond, to challenge the systemic injustices of Jim Crow. A pivotal moment occurred when we visited the zoo in Memphis and faced down a police officer with a drawn weapon. We were told that it wasn't Thursday—the designated day for Black people to visit. This act of defiance against the status quo planted the seeds for my ongoing activism.

At Lincoln University, I continued to be a voice for change. My involvement with local protests and activism gained attention from Roy Wilkins, head of the National Association for the Advancement of Colored People (NAACP). In my senior year, I had the privilege of meeting him, and he offered me the position of Field Representative for the NAACP. My dedication to justice, equality, and civil rights continued into my professional life in the music industry, where I found ways to merge my passion for social justice with my career.

In 1971, while at Capitol Records in Hollywood, I was able to persuade the company to participate in a fundraiser for the Mufundi Institute in California. This was just the beginning of my work in merging the worlds of music and social activism.

At Mercury Records in Chicago, I collaborated with figures such as Rev. Jesse Jackson and Operation Bread Basket, ensuring that artists, and musicians like Melba Moore, Buddy Miles, Gene Chandler, Cannonball Adderley, Jerry Butler, Nancy Wilson, Lou Rawls, MJQ used their platform to support community causes. These were artists that I was working with and were socially conscious. I personally escorted them to the Saturday morning meetings. I also launched a program with Dr. Andrew Thomas called Project 75, which was designed to more than double the number of Black students in medical school by year 1975.

During my time at CBS Records in New York, I helped organize and co-produce a major concert at Mount Morris Park (now Malcolm X

CHAPTER 19: REFLECTIONS

Park) in Harlem, featuring the O'Jays and a star-studded jazz lineup led by Charlie Mingus. Later, I worked on a fundraiser for the Martin Luther King Jr. Center in Atlanta, Georgia, featuring acts like Sly Stone and Albert King. This event was made even more memorable by the attendance of Georgia Governor Jimmy Carter and civil rights leader Andrew Young, and hosted by Mrs. Coretta Scott King, all sponsored by CBS.

One of the defining moments of my career came when I was instrumental in planning the Jackson 5's first trip to Dakar, Senegal. I had the honor of meeting the President of Senegal and later I was appointed as the Ambassador to Senegal for music. As a result of my involvement in Senegal, I was transferred to the International Division of CBS's Paris office, where I helped foster international relations through music.

My work also included teaming up with Harold Sims, a Booker T. Washington graduate and top Black at Johnson Products, in planning a major fundraiser supporting the Black Caucus in Washington, D.C. I co-produced this fundraiser at the Hilton Hotel in Washington, D.C. along with Jo Bridges, an executive from Stax Records. The headliner was Isaac Hayes, with Don Cornelius as the M.C., all sponsored by CBS. I also had an office in Lagos, Nigeria. My assignment also included researching the possibility of CBS establishing a presence there in Black Africa.

While there, I met and spent a lot of time with Fela, Francis Oladele, and other top music artists in Nigeria. Fela's life was presented as a Broadway musical produced by Jay-Z, Jada Pinkett Smith, and Will Smith. Francis Oladele was also considered as a possible joint venture partner for CBS there in Nigeria. Francis Oladele was the first filmmaker in Nigeria and he produced a film with Ossie Davis called *Kongi's Harvest*.

Francis also accompanied me on a trip to Jamaica to study the music scene there because it was so similar to Nigeria. There is a museum in Lagos that includes Francis Oladele, and Geri and I are in several pictures with Francis and his family.

I also did research in Kenya and studied the music scene there. Kenya was not completely foreign to me because I had observed the COGIC members from Kenya who attended the annual church meeting in Memphis every year. I was familiar with the oppression that they had endured under the British. I knew about Jomo Kenyatta and the Kikuyu Tribe.

Don Cornelius, Logan Westbrooks, & Dick Griffey

In July of 1975, I resigned from CBS International Record Company, and moved to Los Angeles, California. I teamed up with Don Cornelius and Dick Griffey in forming Soul Train Records.

I also turned to real estate and invested in properties in Los Angeles. With the guidance of broker Joe Bradfield, my wife Geri and I purchased several properties, including a twenty-four-unit complex.

Our investments went on to include a shopping center known as the Crenshaw Square, where we launched the "Every Sunny Sunday" art show, offering Black artists a prestigious space to showcase their work. We also employed local youth at the shopping center, contributing to the community in multiple ways.

CHAPTER 19: REFLECTIONS

The Crenshaw Square Mall in Los Angeles, owned by Logan & Geri Westbrooks in the 1970s

Logan and Geri Westbrooks Crenshaw Square Mall proprietors and hosts of Every Sunny Sunday Art Show

Every Sunny Sunday Art Show

In 2019 I was notified by the city of Los Angeles that our ownership of the Crenshaw Square mall had been noted on an historical marker in Crenshaw Square at 3840 Crenshaw Blvd.

Historical Marker

CHAPTER 19: REFLECTIONS

This is one of many historical markers throughout the city that lists the contributions of various citizens and cultures. I produced a short video about it starring Alpha Anderson, one of the original Soul Train dancers.

Every Sunny Sunday news article

Alpha Anderson is featured in a video short titled "Step by Step @ LA." It's a video profile of our ownership of Crenshaw Square in the 1970s

Alpha Anderson is featured in a video short titled "Step by Step @ LA." It's a video profile of our ownership of Crenshaw Square in the 1970s.

Geri was a teacher at a boy's camp for delinquent youth for twenty-nine years.

She observed how many of the boys had gone through the foster care system and group homes. We then considered that maybe if we opened a group home for boys, we could prevent them from ending up in a boy's camp. Thus, the idea of opening up a group home was born.

Westbrooks Helping Hands Home for Boys which was located at 3741 West 27th St. in Los Angeles, CA

"Helping Hands Home for Boys," was the name selected, and over the course of fifteen years, we cared for over 400 boys, providing them with a safe space to learn, grow, and thrive.

Each year for my birthday on August 28, the boys planned a birthday party for me. I treasure those days and hold it as a fond memory.

CHAPTER 19: REFLECTIONS

Logan Westbrooks' birthday party at Helping Hands Home for Boys. Circa 1988

While operating Helping Hands Home for Boys and teaching at Camp Miller Kilpatrick, Geri and two coaches decided to create a football team for the boys. Geri set forth academic requirements and Coach Sean Porter and Malcolm Moore provided the challenge and rewards of competitive sports.

The movie *The Gridiron Gang* is based on the true story of these sports and academic programs that my wife directly impacted. The movie starred Dwayne "The Rock" Johnson and Xzibit and came out in 2006. It was produced by Columbia Pictures and distributed by Sony.

After fifteen years of service, we transferred operations and ownership of Helping Hands Home for Boys to Father Flannigan's "Boys Town," which was expanding in Los Angeles.

Geri Westbrooks on the set of The Gridiron Gang
Photo: BRE Magazine October 2006

CHAPTER 19: REFLECTIONS

The Rock, Geri and Logan Westbrooks

The #1 box office film in its opening week September 15, "Gridiron Gang," starring The Rock and Xzibit, is based on a true story.

The Rock, Geri and Logan Westbrooks on the set of The Gridiron Gang. Photo: BRE Magazine Oct. 2006

In addition to our community work, I pursued a new calling when Pastor Benjamin Crouch of Christ Memorial Church encouraged me to enter the ministry.

I followed that advice and was eventually appointed as the pastor of Freewill Missionary COGIC in Monrovia, California, which I later renamed Faith Temple COGIC, and moved the church to Azusa, California. My path in the ministry deepened, and I now serve as the administrative assistant to the jurisdictional bishop, as well as the Executive Secretary of the Jurisdiction.

In my later years, I wrote several books, including *Anatomy of a Record Company: How to Survive the Record Business*, *The Anatomy of the Music Business: How the Game Was & How the Game Has Changed*, and *Power 101: The Harvard Report, Soul Music and The American Dream*. These works are my attempt to share the wisdom gained over decades of experience in both the music and business worlds.

Niece Mary Hines, sisters Shirley & Pearl accompany Logan Westbrooks at Fox 2 TV station St. Louis, Mo. Nov. 9, 2015

CHAPTER 19: REFLECTIONS

Looking back, I am proud of the legacy I've built, one of hard work, dedication, and love for others. From my humble beginnings in Lauderdale Sub on Carnegie Street in South Memphis, Tennessee, I've lived a life rooted in faith, family, and service.

The Westbrooks family 2014: Son in law Jeremy Moxey, grandchildren Jordan, Emelia Hart, Elliott, Brienne, and daughter Babette. Front: Geri and Logan Far Right

As I reflect on my children and grandchildren, Babette, my daughter, and Jeremy, her husband, their children Brienne, Jordan, Elliott, and Emilia Hart, as well as my first great-grandson Arthur, I see a new generation carrying the torch forward.

My granddaughter Jordan is a medical doctor, a PhD candidate, and a rising pop singer. My grandson Elliott is now a pilot and represents the legacy of perseverance and ambition. Emilia Hart, my youngest grandchild, warms my heart with her kindness, joy, and great aptitude.

*Babette Westbrooks Moxey and Logan Westbrooks
St. Louis, MO. May 10, 1992*

*Jeremy, Elliott, and Babette Moxey. Worcester, England,
2016. Elliott graduated with honors with a BS in geography
St. Louis, MO. May 10, 1992*

CHAPTER 19: REFLECTIONS

Elliott Moxey, grandson of Logan and Geri Westbrooks, son of Jeremy Moxey and Babette Westbrooks Moxey

Dr. Jordan Moxey, MD, granddaughter of Logan and Geri Westbrooks, daughter of Jeremy Moxey and Babette Westbrooks Moxey, honors graduate of the University of Birmingham, BS Medical Science & Biomedical Sciences, Bachelor of Medicine and Surgery

Emelia Hart Moxey, granddaughter of Logan and Geri Westbrooks, daughter of Jeremy Moxey and Babette Westbrooks Moxey, honors graduate of University of Worcester. B.A. in Criminology 2022

Jeremy Moxey with daughters Emelia Hart, Brienne, and Jordan. Granddaughters of Logan and Geri Westbrooks Briene's wedding to Timothy James Hodgetts. Wolverhampton, England

CHAPTER 19: REFLECTIONS

Granddaughter Brienne and husband Timothy James Hodgetts with their son Arthur, the first great-grandchild of Logan and Geri Westbrooks. Brienne is a graduate of Staffordshire University with a BS in Business Management 2004

Brienne, Timothy James Hodgetts, Logan and Geri Westbrooks

Westbrooks Family collage, with Logan and Geri Westbrooks

To my children and grandchildren, may you follow your dreams with the same unwavering determination, and know that my thoughts and prayers will always be with you. Though the road you walk may be different, never forget the strength of your roots in Lauderdale Sub. Stay true to yourself, pursue excellence, and continue to build a future that honors the sacrifices and legacy of those who came before you.

For all that this book does not contain, my life's work is preserved in the Archives of African American Music and Culture at the University of Indiana in Bloomington, Indiana.

CHAPTER 20

REVERSAL OF FORTUNE

I'm very proud of how members from the Lauderdale Sub community rose above poverty and racism to achieve success and abundance in Memphis and the world. This was done by never losing faith and by fighting for our rights until we achieved hard-won progress.

The story of the Lauderdale Sub community is a testament to the power of unity, faith, and activism. This moment is proof of what can be achieved when communities come together and when the power of solidarity outshines any obstacles that may stand in the way.

A spirit of community and activism has been foundational for me my whole life. In 2008 my wife and I designated one of our Los Angeles properties as a campaign call center to elect Democrat Barack Obama, our nation's first African American President of the United States.

Obama was qualified indeed and the fact that he was a man of color made the victory even more rewarding. It was something that I never thought I would live to see.

Obama's two successful terms stirred the underbelly of racism and White supremacy. A brash and controversial tyrant was gaining political power.

In 2017, America ushered in the first administration of President #45. This win for the Republican party brought four years of scandal and political chaos.

Mrs. Geri Westbrooks at the Obama Call Center hosted by the Westbrooks in 2008

The Westbrooks' Obama Call Center

CHAPTER 20: REVERSAL OF FORTUNE

44th President of the United States Barack H. Obama with Logan and Geri Westbrooks at a private event

An aging former Vice President Joe Biden entered the race for the presidency in 2020. It was an attempt to preserve our nation's democracy.

Biden won and his victory was challenged for the next four years. #45 (also known as Donald Trump) was not satisfied. He wanted to rule the nation once more. Smeared in lawsuits and thirty-four felony counts, #45 re-entered the presidential race in an effort to be the 47th President of the United States. Biden was willing to run for reelection but at eighty-one years old, his declining stamina was evident. Meanwhile #45 laid out his plan to roll back civil rights, voting rights, birthright citizenship and a litany of other unconstitutional atrocities. They were outlined in his administration's push for Project 2025.

Late summer 2024, President Biden dropped out of the race for reelection and endorsed Vice President Kamala Harris as his nominee. There were skeptics in the Democratic Party, but the stakes were also high. They needed an opponent who could defeat Donald Trump. Vice President Harris chose Minnesota Governor Tim Walz as her running mate and the campaign took off like a meteor.

Once again, my wife and I designated our property located at 5th and Washington Boulevard in Los Angeles to be an official call center, this time to help elect the first Black woman President of the United States in the 2024 election.

We did this with the support of Grassroots Democrats HQ. We even commissioned a mural by Dylan Keene to enshrine the historic moment.

Mural artist Dylan Keene and Dr. Logan H. Westbrooks at 1904 5th Avenue, Los Angeles, CA 90018. In 2024 it was designated as the Harris for President Call Center

CHAPTER 20: REVERSAL OF FORTUNE

Pictured on the mural: Shirley Chisolm, Dr. Martin Luther King Jr., Pres. Barack Obama, V.P. Kamala Harris, Mayor Tom Bradley, Cesar Chavez, Mayor Karen Bass, and Michelle Obama. 2025

In the final analysis, Trump garnered 77.1 million votes and Harris earned 74.7 million votes. That's 49.9% Trump and 48.3% Harris according to Reuters.com. Trump reported a much wider margin of triumph. Still, Kamala Harris got closer to victory than any other female candidate and any candidate of Jamaican and South Asian descent.

LaRita Shelby interviews Dr. Logan Westbrooks about the Harris for President campaign and his history of political activism. September 2024

Along with the help of LaRita Shelby, Robert Harris, and Reggie Simon, we documented our call center into a film titled *Freedom's Pathway Forward*. It won an award in the Filmfare India International Film Festival in Mumbai, India in May of 2025 and the Audience Choice Award at the Pulling Focus Film Festival in Davenport, Iowa in June of 2025.

Kamala Harris warned Americans of Trump's plans under Project 2025. In his first 100 his executive orders proved to be driven by a radical agenda rooted in extreme Christian nationalism.

Trump and the MAGA (Make America Great Again) Republicans are determined to dismantle the very principles of equality and justice. The deliberate targeting of minority communities, Black people, immigrants, women, disabled individuals, and the LGBTQ community through policies that disregard Diversity, Equity, and Inclusion (DEI) represents a direct assault on the values that have shaped this nation's progress. This is a stark reminder that the progress made is never guaranteed.

The firing of qualified individuals to replace them with less-qualified White men, the cutting of DEI programs, the defunding of Historically Black Colleges and Universities (HBCUs) are not isolated actions. They form part of a broader agenda to erode the foundations of diversity and to reinforce a system where only White men hold power, influence, and authority.

Perhaps one of the most profound threats that Project 2025 represents is the looming dismantling of the Voting Rights Act. If the right to vote is stripped away, what's left is a government that would no longer represent the will of the people, but the will of the powerful few. The executive branch, unchecked, could undo decades of civil rights victories, taking us backward in a way that threatens not only the political landscape but the very essence of American democracy.

CHAPTER 20: REVERSAL OF FORTUNE

This shift would induce the divide between the "Haves" and the "Have Nots," increasing inequality in ways that would leave the most vulnerable even more disenfranchised. The erosion of social safety nets, the disregard for human dignity, and the rise of wealth-based privilege would set the stage for a reality where many Americans are left fighting for their basic rights all over again.

The stakes couldn't be higher, and the fear that these shifts could result in the complete reversal of progress made is very real. In this moment of uncertainty, it's essential for us to recognize that the path forward is one that requires collective action. Whether it's through organizing, voting, mobilizing protests, or pressuring lawmakers to protect and expand civil rights, the fight for equality cannot stop. Communities must not lose sight of the core principles that fueled their struggle for justice and equity. Instead, we must continue to amplify our voices, build coalitions, and demand that every individual's humanity is recognized and respected.

If these backward policies succeed in erasing the gains made by marginalized communities, then the responsibility to push back falls on those of us who believe in democracy, fairness, and justice.

We must resist this attempt at resegregation, which is basically a return to segregation also known as Jim Crow.

That was an extremely dark and fearful period in America when Blacks and Whites were separated by color in neighborhoods, schools, restaurants, drinking fountains, buses, and most things in ordinary life. Protests became legendary such as the Montgomery bus boycott, the March across the Edmond Pettis Bridge, and the March on Washington. Unfortunately, it also led to the assassination of several Black leaders such as Martin Luther King Jr., Malcolm X, Medgar Evers, and countless others.

People must rise again, as we did in the past, to demand that America be a place where every citizen—regardless of race, background, gender, or identity—has the same opportunities, the same voice, and the same dignity.

The fight isn't over.

It never was.

So, the struggle continues…

FAMILY PHOTO GALLERY

The wedding reception of Logan and Geri Westbrooks July 10, 1965. Left to Right: Alphonso Sr., Logan, Geri, mother Erma Westbrooks and Geri's mother Tenise Douthet

Erma Westbrooks at Logan and Geri Westbrooks home in Sherman Oaks, California 1971

Goddard Leiberson CBS Records President, Geri Westbrooks, Cheryl Applin (Logan's assistant at CBS) Manhattan, NY 1972

Kathy Sledge Logan, Geri Westbrooks, and Soul Train legend Don Cornelius 1973

Father Peters from Boys Town Nebraska, Publicist Pat Tobin, Producer Chas Johnson, Geri Westbrooks, and Wendel Bates

FAMILY PHOTO GALLERY

*New Memphis Mayor Willie Herenton is congratulated by
Geri & Logan Westbrooks and other guests at
his inauguration in 1992*

*Logan & Geri Westbrooks and Muhammad Ali at a fundraiser
in Las Vegas in 1977*

Sen. Ted Kennedy, Geri Westbrooks, Mrs. Ted Kennedy, and Logan Westbrooks at the home of Clarence & Jackie Avant. Logan Westbrooks Feb 7, 1993

Logan and Geri Westbrooks, Olga James Adderley (Actress from Carmen Jones), Willis Edwards (NAACP) and John Mack (Urban League) at the grand opening of the Crenshaw Square Art Show

FAMILY PHOTO GALLERY

Logan Westbrooks, female guest, former Los Angeles Laker Jamaal Wilkes, Geri and Earl Abdullah, also known as "Earl the Pearl" radio DJ from KJLH 102.3 FM

Geri and Logan greet recording artist Sherrie Payne at book signing for Anatomy of the Music Industry 2015

A charity group of actresses under the name of The Kwanza Foundation raised funds in support of women and youth suffering abuse. Pictured Left-Right: Emily Yancy, Fay Hauser Price, Beverly Todd, Marguerite Ray, Ella Reid, Lisa Jones, and Agnes Talley. Logan & Geri (center) present a donation to Marguerite Ray

FAMILY PHOTO GALLERY

Geri Westbrooks at home in Sherman Oaks, CA

Logan and Geri Westbrooks, Cecil Holmes

Logan and Geri Westbrooks at the White House Christmas party during the Obama Era

Linda and Glodean James (Love Unlimited), Geri and two guests at the White House Christmas party

FAMILY PHOTO GALLERY

Logan and Geri Westbrooks give welcome remarks Freedom's Pathway Forward mural and Kamala Harris for President Call Center while Chas Johnson (3rd from left), Olu Oreduba (center) and Sherrie and Freda Payne look on. 2024

L to R: Jackson Brown, TV producer Chas Johnson, Sherrie Payne, Carolyn Flowers, Celestine Palmer, Geri & Logan Westbrooks, Pastor James McKnight, volunteer from Grassroots Dems, Freda Payne, Mike Davis and Ingrid Van Eckert, VP of Grassroots Dems HQ. Sept 2024

JC McGraw, Logan Westbrooks, Gil Robertson, Oz Moore at The Obama Lounge set up at 5th & Washington Blvd. in LA

Freedoms Pathway Forward Call Center opening reception. Chris Jones, Jordan Patterson, Oz Moore, Sherrie & Freda Payne, JC McGraw, Sam Herenton & Rodney Herenton Jr. Sept 2024

Logan and Geri Westbrooks

Logan and Geri traveled the world

L to R: Toshiko Bowen (Joseph Bowen's wife), Shirley Westbrooks Smith, Alphonso Westbrooks Sr., Gloria Westbrooks, Mrs. Erma Bowen Westbrooks, Alphonso Westbrooks Jr., Alice Westbrooks, Callie May Bowen Lynch, Pearl Westbrooks Hines. On the floor: Little Mary Hines, Geri & Logan Westbrooks.

Alice Moore Westbrooks, the Moxey family with Geri Westbrooks. Wolverhampton, England

FAMILY PHOTO GALLERY

Alphonso Westbrooks Jr. and Mrs. Alice Westbrooks at the Inauguration of President Bill Clinton January 20, 1993

Alice Westbrooks, wife of Alphonso Jr., with multiple generations of the Westbrooks Smith and Hines family

Alicia Westbrooks, daughter of Alphonso Jr. and Alice Westbrooks

Mary Hines. Alicia Westbrooks, Shirley Westbrooks Smith, and Pearl Westbrooks Hines

FAMILY PHOTO GALLERY

Left: Chaz Westbrooks, son of Alicia, grandson of Alphonso Jr. Alpha Westbrooks, daughter of Alice and Alphonso Jr. Right: Jonathan Edward Allen, husband of Alpha Westbrooks

Chaz Westbrooks (2019), son of Alicia, grandson of Alphonso and Alice Westbrooks Jr., great-grandson of Alphonso Westbrooks Sr. and Erma Bowen Westbrooks, great-nephew of Dr. Logan H. Westbrooks

Aricka Westbrooks, daughter of Alphonso Jr. and Alice Westbrooks

Tony Anderson, husband of Aricka Westbrooks Anderson

Left: Adan Anderson, son of Aricka Westbrooks Anderson and Tony Anderson. Right: Anthony Anderson, Stepson of Aricka, and son of Tony Anderson

The Andersons are the owners of Jive Turkey, specializing in deep fried turkeys. 332 Myrtle Ave. New York, NY 11205

Standing: AJ & Michael Moore, Michelle (wife of Michael), Brandon, Michael Moore, Reggie Smith, Mary Hines. Seated: Rosie Tatum (grandmother to Reginald Smith, Jr.), Shirley Westbrooks Smith, Regina Smith Patrick, Pearl Westbrooks Hines

Alfred Michael Moore II, son of Gloria Westbrooks Moore (Center) and Bernice Bowen Jones sister of Erma Bowen Westbrooks

FAMILY PHOTO GALLERY

Michelle Moore, Alfred Michael Moore III (AJ), Ryan Moore, Brandon Moore, and Alfred Michael Moore II

Dr. Reginald Floyd Smith II, Executive Director of the Urban League of Chattanooga, TN, grandmother Shirley Westbrooks Smith, and Chemical Engineer Mrs. Regina Smith Patrick, wife of Brandon Patrick

Reginald Smith Sr., son of Shirley Westbrooks Smith

Regina A. Smith Patrick (daughter of Reginald Smith Sr., granddaughter of Shirley Westbrooks Smith) and her husband Brandon Patrick. Logan is presiding.

Dr. Reginald Smith Jr. II, PhD, Mrs. Kimberly Smith, and their children Reginald III and Katherine, grandson and great grandchildren of Shirley Westbrooks Smith

Patrick and Regina Smith, Bryleigh Rose (3 yrs) and Baileigh Regina (1 yr)

Pearl, Shirley, Geri, and Logan. Christmas 2016

Pearl Westbrooks Hines and brother Alphonso Westbrooks Jr.

Left: Mary Hines, daughter of Pearl Westbrooks Hines (far right), and Shirley Westbrooks Smith (Center)

FAMILY PHOTO GALLERY

Pearl Hines and daughter Mary. Below: Son, Robert Hines III

Robert Hines III and son Justin Hines
Son and grandson of Pearl Westbrooks Hines

FAMILY PHOTO GALLERY

Justin and Robert Hines III graduation 2022

The Westbrooks and Moxey Family

Babette Westbrooks Moxey

The Moxey Family

FAMILY PHOTO GALLERY

Emelia Hart Moxey and fiancé William James Gibbons

Dr. Maya Jordan Moxey has found a love for music.

Elliott Moxey and his wife Hanna

Arthur Hodgetts, son of Brienne Moxey and Timothy James Hodgetts (Born April 14, 2022), great-grandson of Logan and Geri Westbrooks

Dr. Logan H. Westbrooks receiving the Music Pioneer Award, 2015

Babette Westbrooks worked at Source Records with William Earl Hicks and Jaunese Allen in the summer of 1981

Logan Westbrooks, Mayor Kenneth Gibson and recording artist Jerry Butler

John Buchanan — Richardo Wellman — Jerry Wilder — Chuck Brown (sitting) — LeRoy Fleming — Gregory Gerran — Curtis Johnson — Donald Tillery

Chuck Brown and The Soul Searchers

Exclusively On SOURCE
MCA RECORDS

Rev. Billy Kyles, Al Bell, Logan Westbrooks, and Isaac Hayes

Logan Westbrooks presents his first gold record on Source Records (Bustin' Loose by Chuck Brown and the Soul Searchers) MCA Universal President Lew Wasserman. Norbert Simmons, Pres. MCA New Ventures (pictured left) and Sidney Steinberg is far right. Los Angeles, CA 1980

Logan Westbrooks presentsa Gold Album on behalf of the Jackson family to President and Mrs. Abdou Diouf President of Senegal in Dakar West Africa. A staff interpretor is pictured 2nd from left. 1997

Logan Westbrooks, Coretta Scott King and United Nations Ambassador Andrew Young at a MLK Center fundraiser

Tom Nixon producer for Stax Records (standing), Dr. Benjamin Hooks (rear). Seated: Al Jackson, Revé Gipson, Logan & Geri Westbrooks, Al Jackson's wife. Seated in front: Jo Bridges from Stax Records

Henry Grey, local businessman from Chicago, and his wife. Dr. Andrew Thomas from the National Medical Association in Boston, MA, and Logan Westbrooks. Logan receives an Award of Recognition for his participation in Project 75. They are pictured at the 1975 National Medical Association convention in Boston, Massachusetts.

Note: *During his career as a record executive, Logan Westbrooks was instrumental in organizing massive fundraising campaigns to support Black students in medical school.*

FAMILY PHOTO GALLERY

Harold Melvin and Teddy Pendergrass celebrate their first gold record

Westbrooks and Don Cornelius beam with happiness at the playback of the Soul Train Theme

Westbrooks presents gold records to the Blue Notes and their producers

A wall of platinum and gold in Logan Westbrooks' home office in Sherman Oaks, CA

FAMILY PHOTO GALLERY

Logan Westbrooks presents Billboard Award to industry godfather Clarence Avant

Logan and Geri Westbrooks living life to the fullest

FAMILY PHOTO GALLERY

Source Records display at the University of Indiana Archives of African American Music and Culture in Bloomington, Indiana

In 2013 Lincoln University alums Dr. Troy Davis and Dr. Logan Westbrooks commissioned a docu-short film about the founding of Lincoln University by soldiers from the 62nd and 65th Colored infantry and the White soldiers who supported the effort. The film was written & directed by LaRita Shelby and starred Erich Hicks, Roscoe Freeman, Reginald T. Dorsey as Buffalo soldiers with Max Thayard as President Lincoln and Tony Winters as the butler

FAMILY PHOTO GALLERY

Dr. Logan H. Westbrooks

FAMILY PHOTO GALLERY

LaRita Shelby & Co-host Jay Styles

Your Hollywood Local was produced by Logan Westbrooks and hosted by co-producer, writer & director LaRita Shelby with co-hosts Jay Styles and Justin Key in 2017

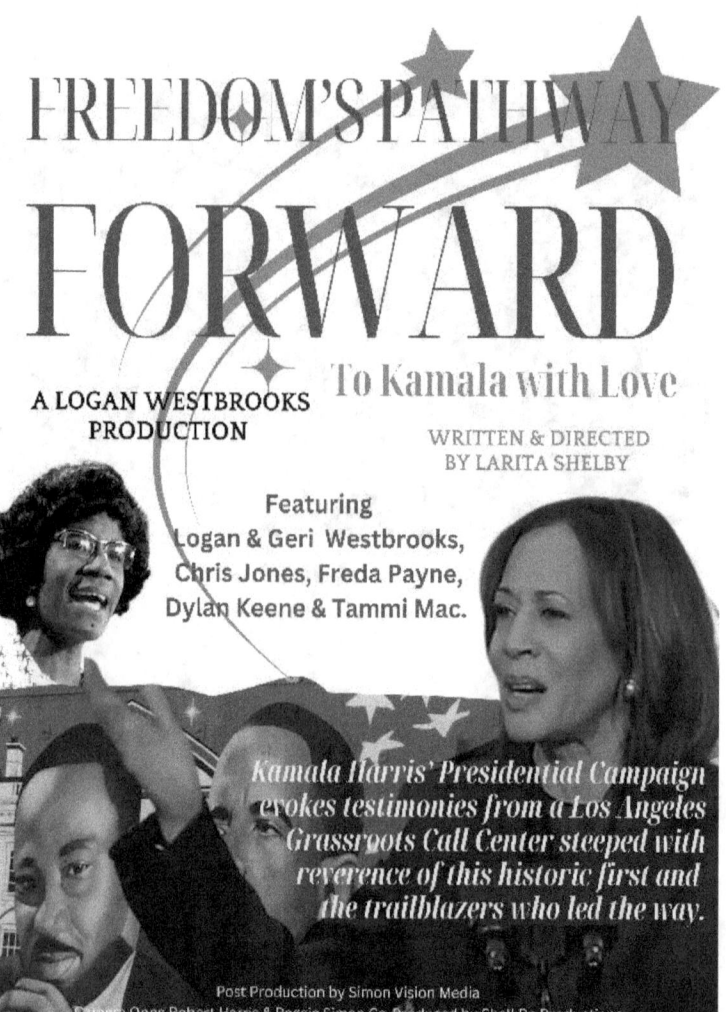

FAMILY PHOTO GALLERY

Dr. Logan H. Westbrooks' collection of records, memorandums, photographs, awards, and other artifacts are permanently housed at the University of Indiana's Archives of African American Music and Culture in Bloomington, Indiana. They are also available online at www.archives.iu.edu

Dr. & Mrs. Westbrooks with Dr. Portia Maultsby, who was instrumental in setting up the Logan Westbrooks Collection at the University of Indiana

Shirley, Logan and Pearl share laughter and memories at an event in 2019

FAMILY PHOTO GALLERY

The original concept for the cover of the book focused on the evolution of the Westbrooks family. We ultimately chose a cover that was inclusive of the community at large

Education was always key for the Westbrooks family. Dr. Westbrooks is seen here speaking at Nelly's school in St. Louis, Mo. 2015

Dr. Westbrooks speaking at Indiana University 2013

LAUDERDALE SUB PHOTO GALLERY

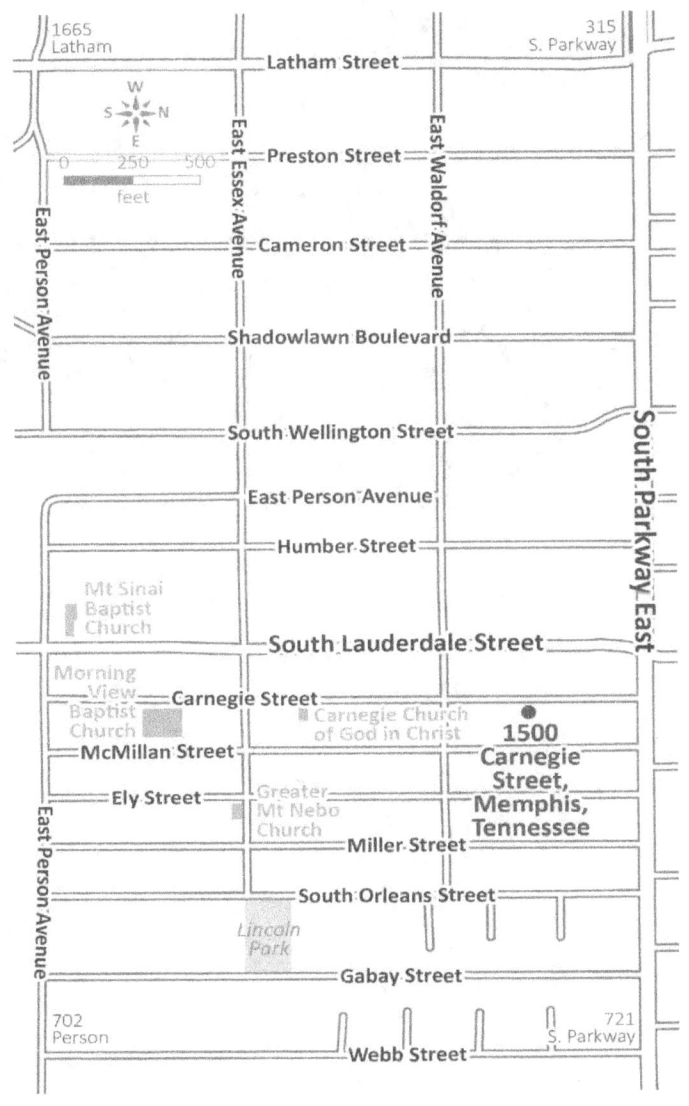

Willie Mitchell Studios at 1320 Lauderdale has been renamed Willie Mitchell Boulevard in the 1300 block. It is now a historic landmark. It was previously The Shamrock Theater, which opened in 1915 for Whites only. In 1957 it became Royal Studios, home of Hi Records and the Hi Rhythm Section, curated by famous soul music trumpeter producer Willie Mitchell

LAUDERDALE SUB PHOTO GALLERY

Corner of Parkway and Lauderdale as pictured in 2025. It was formerly a drug store where Logan shined shoes out front during his youth in Lauderdale Sub

Boarded house in Lauderdale Sub 2025

Dilapidated home in Lauderdale Sub 2025

LAUDERDALE SUB PHOTO GALLERY

Home where Logan Westbrooks was born 1400 block of College Street, Memphis, TN

Former home of the Patterson family

LAUDERDALE SUB: MEMORIES OF A MEMPHIS NEIGHBORHOOD

Another abandoned property in Lauderdale Sub

Occupied house in Lauderdale Sub 2025

LAUDERDALE SUB PHOTO GALLERY

Lauderdale and Essex

Person and Ely Street

This home at 1665 McMillan Street is still occupied by members of the Hawkins Davenport family in 2025

1658 Carnegie Street is the former residence of the Hawkins family. It was sold to the Givens Hardy family in 1990. It stands well-kept and on solid ground in 2025

Though most of the old neighborhood is blighted, these and a few other homes are still standing with family members who are thriving and are proud residents of Lauderdale Sub. Their descendants continue to make their mark on the world!

INDEX

SYMBOLS

1960 Memphis Sit-In Movement, The 93

A

Abbott, Robert S. 180
Abbott Scholarship 180
Abdullah, Earl (a.k.a Earl the Pearl)
    Photos: 233
Abdullah, Geri
    Photos: 233
Ace Theater 29
Adderley, Cannonball 202
Adderley, Olga James
    Photos: 232
African American Baptist Church 83
Aiden (surname unknown) 158
Alexander, Lamar 102
Allen, David, Jr. 69
Allen, Fredericka Laverne
    Photos: 72
Allen, George Robert 76
Allen, Jaunese
    Photos: 261
Allen, Jonathan Edward
    Photos: 243
Allen, Maurine Delores 76
Allen, Merle 72
Allen, Rance 108
Allen, Sammie Steen 76
Allen (surname unknown) 117
Allen, Willie B. 72
Allen, Willie Merle 76
Alpha Kappa Alpha Sorority 139
Alumni Hall of Fame Healing House, The 17
American Heart Association 117
American Lebanese Syrian Associated Charities (ALSAC) 67
Anatomy of a Record Company 1 & 2 14, 17, 212
Anatomy of the Music Industry: How the Game Was & How the Game Has Changed, The 17
Anderson, Adan
    Photos: 245
Anderson, Alpha 207
    Photos: 207
Anderson, Anthony
    Photos: 245
Anderson, Aricka Westbrooks 245
    Photos: 244
Anderson, Mother 188
Anderson, Ronald 3, 4
Anderson, Sister 149, 150
Anderson, Tony 244, 245
Applin, Cheryl

Photos: 229
Archives of African American Music and Culture at the University of Indiana 218
Ascent Books 17
Ashley (surname unknown), Davenport Family 50
Atlanta Daily World
Audience Choice Award 224
Austin, Marcia Washington Seymour 69
Avant, Clarence
Photos: 269
Avant, Jackie
Photos: 232
Avery Chapel 124, 130
Azusa Street Revival 106

B

Baptist Young People's Union (BYPU) 193
Barry, Marion 93, 202
Bass, Karen
Photos: 223
Bates, Wendel
Photos: 230
Bell, Al
Photos: 263
Bethel Presbyterian Church 200
Beulah Baptist Church 160
Bibb, Mr. 97
Biden, Joe 221
Birmingham World, The 141
Bishop, Jesse Henry Joseph, Sr. 37
Bishop, Memory Austin 37
Black, Carrie Mae Moore 81, 82

Photos: 80
BlackThen.com 76
Blake, Bishop Charles S. 33
Blake, Bishop Charles Sr. 151
Photos: 152
Boatner, Barbara Joyce 106
Bobo Family, The 23
Bogart, Humphrey 81
Bolden, P. S.
Photos: 178
Bond, Betty
Photos: 53
Bond, Vivian
Photos: 53
Booker T. Washington High School 5, 12, 30, 31, 39, 43, 61, 77, 92, 101, 138, 139, 143, 160, 179, 180
Photos: 178
Borders, Benny 196
Borders, Mary Ann 9
Photos: 195
Borders, Rosie Lee 196
Bowen, Callie May
Photos: 240
Bowen, Charles
Photos: 140
Bowen, Erma Jean
Photos: 171
Bowen, Horace
Photos: 173
Bowen, Joseph 166
Photos: 174, 240
Bowen, Rose
Photos: 171
Bowen, Toshiko
Photos: 240
Bradfield, Joe 204
Bradford, Sammie Steen Allen 76

Bradley, Tom
Photos: 223
Brandon, Michelle
Photos: 246
Broadnax, Gladys Greene
Photos: 113
Brown, Garnett (a.k.a. Tut) 29, 95, 148
Photos: 93
Brown, Jackson
Photos: 237
Brown, Jean Francois 93
Brown, Margaret Ann 29, 93, 94, 148
Brown, Samuel 93
Bryant, Beatrice 41, 42
Bryant, Brenda 42
Bryant, Charles 42, 43
Bryant, Donald 2, 29
Photos: 42, 149
Bryant, Edward, Jr. 42
Bryant, Edward Sr. 42
Bryant, Elon 42
Bryant, Gene 42
Bryant, Jamie 42
Bryant, Kenneth 42
Bryant, Margie
Photos: 41, 42
Bryant, Tina 42
Butler, Jerry 13, 186, 202
Photos: 261
BYPU (Baptist Young People's Union) 193

C

Campbell, Lucie 54
Camp Miller Kilpatrick 209
Capitol Records 12, 13, 184, 185, 202
Caring Hearts Day Care Center 164, 166
Carnegie Church of God in Christ 26, 28, 41, 63, 142, 174, 188, 189
Photos: 141, 187
Carter, Jimmy 14, 203
CBS 13, 14, 15, 186, 202, 203, 204, 229
CBS Records 13, 15, 202, 229
Chandler, Gene 13, 186, 202
Chavez, Cesar
Photos: 223
Chisolm, Shirley
Photos: 223
Chuck Brown & the Soul Searchers 16
Church of God in Christ (COGIC) 16, 26, 28, 32, 34, 41, 63, 104, 105, 106, 107, 112, 113, 114, 124, 141, 142, 151, 152, 158, 160, 174, 175, 176, 187, 188, 189
Claudine (surname unknown), or Claudia 87
Claxton, Rev. Ronald
Photos: 193, 194
Clay Street School 77
Clinton, Bill 34, 158, 241
COGIC (Church of God in Christ) 14, 34, 104, 106, 107, 109, 110, 113, 114, 115, 141, 142, 149, 151, 152, 160, 187, 190, 200, 204, 212
Cole, Kenneth 202
Coleman, Barbara
Photos: 190
Collection at Indiana University's Archives of African American Music and Culture 17

INDEX

Collins, Bessie 81
Collins, David James 82
Columbia Pictures 209
Columbia Records International 15
Commercial Appeal 86, 174, 175
Commonwealth Edison 157
Cooke, Sam 12
Cornelius, Don 13, 15, 203
Photos: 204, 230
Cossitt Library 93
Crawford, Lula Patricia Dunford 117
Crenshaw Square 16, 204, 205, 206, 207, 208, 232
Crouch, Benjamin 16, 204
Photos: 205, 206, 207, 208, 232
Curtis, Helene 157

D

Dandridge, Eddie 30
Daniels, George 13
Dank, Rev. Dr. Reginald Lawrence Porter Sr. 10, 197
Davenport, Addie Arnice 191
Davenport, Addie Westbrook 30, 45, 192
Photos: 49
Davenport, Annie Catherine
Photos: 48
Davenport, Hattie Marie 47, 50, 150
Photos: 48
Davenport, Herbert, Sr. 49
Photos: 48
Davenport, Jake 47, 49, 121
Davenport, Magnolia 49, 121, 122, 126, 127, 129, 132, 150
Photos: 45, 48, 53, 128
Davenport, Rev. Herbert Eugene, Jr. 30, 48

Photos: 48
Davenport, Roneta 48
Photos: 48
Davenport, Roy 48
Davenport, Virginia Hawkins 46, 48, 60, 121, 129, 152
Photos: 47
Davis, Barbara 104
Davis, Clive 13, 186
Davis, Dr. Troy Davis
Photos: 272
Davis, Mike
Photos: 237
Davis, Miles 13, 14
Davis, Ollie
Photos: 96
Davis, Ossie 203
Davis, Sammy, Jr. 94
DeBarge family 16
DEI (Diversity, Equity, and Inclusion) 224
Dempsey, Jack 16
Diamond, Miss 137, 160
Diouf, Abdou 15
Photos: 264
Diouf, Mrs. Abdou
Photos: 264
Discogs 42, 44
District of Columbia Teacher's College 62
Diversity, Equity, and Inclusion (DEI) 224
Dixon, Roscoe 92
Doris, Bobby 75
Doris, Pearl 75
Dorsey, Reginald T.
Photos: 272
Douthet, Geri 11

293

Douthet, Tenise
   Photos: 228
Draper, Tom 182
Drew, Dr. Charles 165
Dukes, Fannie Mae 189
Dunford, Ellen Louise
   Photos: 116
Dunford, Kathleen 117
Dunford, Lula Patricia 117

E

Earlene, Rev. Townes 160
Earl the Pearl (Earl Abdullah)
   Photos: 233
Earth, Wind & Fire 13
Eastern Baptist Seminary 62
Eckert, Ingrid Van
   Photos: 237
Edmond Pettis Bridge 225
Edwards, Martha Jane 85
Edwards, Willis
   Photos: 232
Elks (Improved Benevolent Protective Order of Elks of the World (IBPOEW)) 12, 69, 179, 200
Elks National Oratorical Contest 69
Estes, James 200
Eternal Word Graduate School 16
Evers, Medgar 225

F

Faith Award from Faith Love & Hope Unlimited 17
Father Bertrand High School 62
FCC (Federal Communications Commission) 66, 70
Firestone 56
Fischer Lime and Cement Company 100
   Photos: 101
Fitzgerald, Ella 157
Fleming, Rev. Alvin
   Photos: 193
Flowers, Carolyn
   Photos: 237
Ford, Bishop Louis Henry 158
Ford, Bishop Louis S. 32
Ford Road School 127
Foster, Elder 173
Four Kings, The 43
   Photos: 44
Franklin, Willie Merle Allen 76
Freedom's Pathway Forward 17, 224
   Photos: 237
Freeman, Roscoe
   Photos: 272
Freewill Missionary Church of God in Christ (COGIC) 212
Friendship Baptist Church 30
Fuller Park 193, 197

G

Gardner, Marqueline 69
Gardner's One Stop 13
Garner, Erroll 13, 186
Gassaway, Sadie 76
Gene, Charles 42
George Daniels' Record Store 13
George Washington University 62
Georgia Theater 29
Gibbons, William James
   Photos: 257
Gibbs, Rosie Moore 81
Gibson, Kenneth

INDEX

Photos: 261
Gigafactory of Compute 170
Gilliam Family 23
Gipson, Revé
   Photos: 265
Givens Family 23
Gloryland Deliverance Temple Church of God in Christ (COGIC) 188, 189, 190
   Photos: 187
Golden, Cheryl, PhD
   Photos: 148
Gordon Elementary 102
G. P. Hamilton Scholarship 77
Graceland Junior High School 140
Graham, Billy 107
Grassroots Democrats 222
Greater Mount Nebo Baptist Church 26
Green, Al 29, 95
Greenwood Baptist Church 59
Grey, Henry
   Photos: 266
Gridiron Gang, The 209
   Photos: 210, 211
Griffey, Dick 15, 204
   Photos: 204

H

Hackworth, Bishop J. Bernard
   Photos: 115
Haile, Jackie Ray 69
Haile, Mary Louise 149
   Photos: 154
Haile, Sterling 69
Haile, Sterling Jr. 69
Haley, Corinne 56
Haley, James C. 55, 56

Photos: 55
Haley, Lawrence 57
Haley, Lizzie 55, 56
Hall, Cheryl (a.k.a Cherie) 103
Hamilton Elementary 128, 149
Hamilton, G. P. 77
Hamilton High School 29, 76, 125, 128, 130
Hammond, Allen 202
Hampton, Lionel 148
Hancock, Herbie 13, 14, 29, 148
Harlow, Bennie 200
Harold Melvin & The Blue Notes 14, 16
Harris, Kamala 221, 223, 224
   Photos: 222, 237
Harris Memorial Christian Methodist Episcopal Church 26
Harris, Robert 224
Hart, Brienne 18
   Photos: 213, 216, 217
Hart, Emelia 18
   Photos: 213, 216, 257
Hart, Jordan 18
   Photos: 213
Harvard Report, The 13, 17, 212
Harvard University 13
Havenview School 56
Hawkings, Lord Kelvin 46, 60
Hawkins, Bishop Milton R.
   Photos: 111
Hawkins, Claudia 61, 62, 87, 149, 154
   Photos: 61, 154
Hawkins, Florence 54, 69, 149, 152
   Photos: 53
Hawkins, Floretta (a.k.a Buug) 68, 69, 70, 153
Hawkins, Howard 46, 60

Hawkins, Lieutenant Susie B. 66
Hawkins, Mary Louise Johnson (a.k.a Marylou) 149
Hawkins, Mary Patterson 103, 106, 111, 114
Photos: 104
Hawkins, Ritta 59, 62, 87
Photos: 59, 64
Hawkins, Virginia 46, 47, 48, 49, 60, 121, 129, 152
Photos: 47
Hawkins, Walter Guy 48
Photos: 128
Hawkins, Walter Guy, Sr. (a.k.a Uncle Bud) 46, 52, 129
Hawkins, Willie Gertrude
Photos: 128
Hayes, Isaac 15, 203
Photos: 263
Haymon, Al 15
HBCU (Historically Black Colleges and Universities) 17
Hedgeman, Dr. Lulah 113
Helping Hands Home for Boys 16, 208, 209
Photos: 208, 209
Henderson Business College 85
Herenton, Rodney, Jr.
Photos: 238
Herenton, Sam
Photos: 238
Herenton, Willie 163
Photos: 231
Hicks, Erich
Photos: 272
Hicks, William Earl
Photos: 261
Hines, Justin
Photos: 254
Hines, Lillian
Photos: 53
Hines, Mary
Photos: 212, 240, 242, 246, 252
Hines, Pearl Westbrooks 6
Photos: 159, 240, 242, 246, 251, 252, 254
Hines, Robert III
Photos: 253, 254, 255
History of The Neely Family: Many Homelands, One Family, The 102
Hodges, Fredericka Laverne Allen 5
Photos: 72
Hodgetts, Arthur 18
Photos: 259
Hodgetts, Timothy James
Photos: 216, 217, 259
Holland Dozier Holland Holmes, Rev. 185
Holmes, Cecil
Photos: 235
Home of the Heroes 17
Hooks, Dr. Benjamin
Photos: 265
Hooligans, The 29
Howard, Clarence 49
Howard, Claribelle 49, 122, 126, 127
Photos: 121
Howard, Emma Dee 49
Howard, Magnolia Davenport 121
Photos: 128, 130
Howard, Simon L., Jr. 121, 130
Howard, Simon, Sr. 121
Hoyle, Bernice Moore 82
Hudson, Faye Catherine Neely 100
Hunt, Blair T. 200
Hunt, Blair T., Jr.
Photos: 178

INDEX

I

Ian (surname unknown) 158
Institutional Equity Title IX 69
Isley Brothers 13
It's Never Too Late 17

J

Jackson 5 15, 203
Jackson Gardner, Marq 69, 197
Jackson, Mamie Kate 38
Jackson, Moses 38
Jackson, Rev. Henry
  Photos: 198
Jackson, Rev. Jesse 202
James, Glodean
  Photos: 236
James, Linda
  Photos: 236
Jazz Crusaders, The 148
Jenkins, Rev. M. J. 196
  Photos: 196
Jim Crow 5, 39, 74, 77, 162, 202, 225
Jim Neely's Interstate Bar-B-Que 99
  Photos: 99
Jive Turkey
  Photos: 245
Johnson, Anthony Lamont 69
Johnson, Chas
  Photos: 230, 237
Johnson, Dwayne, (a.k.a 'The Rock') 209
  Photos: 211
Johnson, Jackie Ray, Jr. 154
Johnson, Jeff
  Photos: 148
Johnson, Mary Louise Hawkins 149
  Photos: 154
Johnson Publishing Company 12, 182
Johnson, Rev. John 192
  Photos: 192
Johnson, Sterling, Jr. 69
Jones, Alma
  Photos: 171
Jones, Bernice Bowen
  Photos: 246
Jones, Bishop O. T. 32
Jones, Chris
  Photos: 238
Jones, Lisa
  Photos: 234

K

Katoe, Dorothy Kathleen Stiles 116
Keene, Dylan 222
  Photos: 222
Keeney, Frances 124
Kennedy, Mrs. Ted
  Photos: 232
Kennedy, Ted
  Photos: 232
Kenyatta, Jomo 204
Key, Dr. Justin 11
Kikuyu Tribe 204
King, Albert 203
King, Coretta Scott 14, 203
  Photos: 264
King, Dr. Martin Luther, Jr. 43, 123, 201, 203, 225
  Photos: 223
Kitts, EJ 75
Knox College 62
Koen, Bertha
  Photos: 95
Koen, Delia 11
  Photos: 96
Koen, George 95
  Photos: 95, 96

Koen, Margaret Alice
Photos: 96
Koen, Robert
Photos: 96
Koen's Cleaners
Photos: 96
Kongi's Harvest 203
Kortrecht High School 77
Kuti, Fela 15
KWAM Radio 52, 54
Kwanza Foundation, The
Photos: 234
Kyles, Rev. Billy
Photos: 263

L

Labelle, Patti 13
Lavong, Reggie 185
Laws, Rev. L. L. 196
Photos: 196
Leaks, Rev. R. L., Sr.
Photos: 198
Leaners, The 13
Leiberson, Goddard
Photos: 229
LeMoyne Eight 30, 93
LeMoyne Normal School 37
LeMoyne-Owen College 5, 12, 17, 30, 37, 39, 40, 43, 62, 69, 93, 101, 102, 112, 117, 124, 131, 139, 147, 160, 178, 179, 201
Photos: 36
Lester Elementary 61
Lincoln Elementary School 28, 76, 83, 128, 137, 172
Photos: 137, 161
Lincoln Junior High School 43

Lincoln University 12, 17, 34, 147, 156, 179, 180, 181, 202
Photos: 272
Lipscomb, Robert, MBA
Photos: 148
Living Legends Foundation 17
Logan H. Westbrooks 6, 10, 12, 17, 25, 111, 170, 260, 273, 277
Photos: 26, 148, 222
Logan, Kathy Sledge
Photos: 230
London, Hezekiah 149
Loving and Lifting Caregivers Support Ministry at Saint Andrew African Methodist Episcopal Church 117
Lundvall, Bruce 186
Lutheran Cooperative School 128
Lynch, Callie May Bowen
Photos: 240

M

Mack, John
Photos: 232
Mafundi Institute 13
MAGA (Make America Great Again) 224
Malcolm X 202, 225
Malcolm X Park 202
Manassas High School 61
Marissa (surname unknown), Hawkins Family 70
Marquette University 130
Mars, Bruno 29
Martin, Dr. Judy C. 50
Martin, Dr. Julia 50

INDEX

Martin, Hattie Marie Davenport 47, 50, 150
  Photos: 48
Martin Luther King Jr. Center 203
Martin, Sammie 113
Mason, Bishop Charles Harrison 105, 106
Mason, Deborah Indiana 105
Mason Temple 34
  Photos: 33, 176
Mathis, Johnny 13
Matthews, Addie Arnice Davenport 48, 191
Matthews, Magnolia Davenport (a.k.a Sweet Baby) 132
  Photos: 45, 48, 191
Maultsby, Dr. Portia
  Photos: 278
Mayfield, Brother 200
Maynard, Bishop Jerry L., Sr. 107
McClellan, Mrs. 200
McDaniel, Rev. James A. 200
McDonald, Evelyn 117
McDonald, Henry 117
McEwen, Bishop A. B., Sr. 112
McEwen, Lulah 112
McEwen, Sammie Martin 113
McGraw, JC
  Photos: 238
McKnight, Pastor James
  Photos: 237
McNeal, Dorothy 187
  Photos: 190
McNeal, RC 189
  Photos: 188
McNeal, Robert, Sr. 142
McNeal, Samuel Evans, Jr. 187
McNeal, Samuel Evans, Sr. 189
  Photos: 188
McNeal, Sharyece
  Photos: 190
McNeal, Stephen C. 189
M. E. Carter and Company 84
Meharry Medical College 29, 149
Memphis Blues Hall of Fame 43
Memphis City Schools 102, 150
Memphis Jewels, The 52, 54
Memphis State University 62
Memphis Theological Seminary 62
Memphis World 32, 86, 90, 141, 163, 174, 175, 180
  Photos: 90, 140
Mercury Records 13, 186, 202
Metropolitan Baptist Church 58, 63, 65
Metropolitan Ecclesiastical Jurisdiction of Southern California 16, 147
Miles, Buddy 13, 186, 202
Minette's One Stop 13
Mingus, Charlie 14, 203
Miss Black Memphis 69
Miss Black World 69
Miss Black World of Tennessee 69
Mississippi Boulevard Christian Church 179
Mississippi Industrial College 131
Mitchell, Alfred 57
Mitchell, Angela 197
Mitchell, Mary Ann Borders 9, 195
  Photos: 195
Mitchell, Ricky 197
Moore, AJ
  Photos: 246, 247
Moore, Alfred Michael 170

Moore, Alfred Michael, II
Photos: 246, 247
Moore, Alfred Michael, III (a.k.a AJ)
Photos: 247
Moore, Alice
Photos: 240
Moore, Bernice 82
Moore, Brandon
Photos: 247
Moore, Carrie Mae 81, 82
Photos: 80
Moore, Gloria Westbrooks 246
Moore, Humphrey Taft, Jr. 82
Moore, Humphrey Taft, Sr. 81
Moore, Malcolm 209
Moore, Martha Jane 81, 85
Moore, Melba 13, 186, 202
Moore, Michael
Photos: 246
Moore, Michelle
Photos: 247
Moore, Ola Nell 82
Moore, Oz
Photos: 238
Moore, Peter 82, 148
Moore, Rosie 81
Moore, Ryan
Photos: 247
Moore, Warren 24, 150
Morgan (surname unknown), Hawkins Family 70
Morning View Baptist Church 30, 52, 63, 88, 130, 141, 191, 194
Mount Morris Park 202
Mount Nebo Baptist Church 26
Moxey, Babette Westbrooks 18
Moxey, Brienne 259
Moxey, Elliott 18, 213
Photos: 213, 215, 258
Moxey, Emelia Hart (or 'Emilia') 18, 213
Photos: 213, 216, 257
Moxey, Hanna
Photos: 258
Moxey, Jeremy 18
Photos: 213, 215, 216
Moxey, Jordan, MD
Photos: 215
Moxey, Maya Jordan, MD
Photos: 257
Mr. Kitts 75
Mt. Sinai Missionary Baptist Church 195, 196
Music Pioneer Award, The 17, 260
Musk, Elon 170

N

NAACP (National Association for the Advancement of Colored People) 17, 117, 202
Photos: 232
Nash, Johnny 13
National Association for the Advancement of Colored People (NAACP) 17, 117, 202
Photos: 232
National Association of Television and Radio Announcers (NATRA) 14
National Medical Association 13
Photos: 266
Neely, Barbara
Photos: 31, 95
Neely, Beverly 99, 101
Neely, Delores Ann 100
Neely, Faye Catherine 100

INDEX

Neely, Gloria 101
Neely, Harry 34
Neely, James 2, 32, 89, 99, 101
   Photos: 31, 89
Neely, Jessie 101
Neely, Jim 99, 111
Neely, Patricia 101
Neely, Shirley Claire 100
   Photos: 100
Neely, Stephanie Joy 98
Neely, William Jr. 101
New Daisy 29, 94
Nixon, President 14
Nixon, Tom
   Photos: 265
Non-Commissioned Officer's Club 182

O

Obama, Barack H. 219, 223
   Photos: 221
Obama, Michelle 223
O'Jays, The 13, 203
Oladele, Francis 203, 204
Olivet Baptist Church 97, 101
Ollivierre, Alison 11
Omega Psi Phi Fraternity 17
Omni Coliseum 14
Operation Bread Basket 202
Oreduba, Olu
   Photos: 237
Orpheum Theater 163
Overton High School 113
Owen, Bishop Chandler D.
   Photos: 115
Owen Junior College 93

P

Paige, Sharon 16
Palmer, Celestine
   Photos: 237
Parks, Rosa 118
Patrick, Brandon
   Photos: 249
Patrick, Regina A. Smith
   Photos: 249
Patterson, Barbara 111, 112
Patterson, Bishop G. E. 2, 5, 103, 106, 107, 108, 110, 111
   Photos: 103, 109
Patterson, Bishop Gilbert Earl 33, 95, 114, 151
Patterson, Bishop William Archie, Sr.
   Photos: 104
Patterson, James Oglethorpe, Jr.
   Photos: 105
Patterson, James Oglethorpe, Sr., a.k.a. J. O. 106, 151
   Photos: 105
Patterson, Lee Ella 106, 111, 112
   Photos: 112, 151
Patterson, Mary 103, 106, 111, 114
   Photos: 104
Patterson, William Archie, Sr.
   Photos: 104
Paul, Billy 13
Payne, Freda
   Photos: 237, 238
Payne, Sherrie
   Photos: 233, 237
Peabody Library 93
Peebles, Ann 29, 43
Perry, Quintin 15
Peters, Father
   Photos: 230

Porter, Reginald Jr. 66
Porter, Rev. Davena Young 65
    Photos: 65
Porter, Rev. M. L. 153
Porter, Rev. Reginald Lawrence, Sr.
    (a.k.a Dank) 5, 10, 70, 197
    Photos: 58, 59, 65
Porter, Ritta Hawkins 59, 62, 87
    Photos: 59, 64
Porter, Roderick K., Sr. 62
Porter, Sean 209
Porter, Sonya 66
Power 101: The Harvard Report, Soul Music and The American Dream 212
Presley, Elvis 8, 12, 52, 183, 193
Price, Fay Hauser
    Photos: 234
Progressive National Baptist Convention 66
Project 75 202
    Photos: 266
Pulliam, Miss 193
Pulling Focus Film Festival 224

R

Randolph, Asa Philip 125
Rawls, Lou 202
Ray, Marguerite
    Photos: 234
Reid, Ella
    Photos: 234
Reynolds, Rev. John L. 192
    Photos: 192
Richie, Lionel 29
Roberts, Anna Hubbard 200
Robertson, Gil
    Photos: 238

Robinson, Dee 11
Rose Book Store 13
Rust College 131

S

Saint Andrew African Methodist Episcopal Church 117
Saint Anthony Catholic School 62
Saint Augustine Catholic Church 101, 117
Saint Augustine Catholic School 29, 117
Saint Augustine Elementary 101
Saint John Number One Baptist Church 59
Santana 13
Saunders, Rev. L. D.
    Photos: 192
Scott, Emma Dee Howard 49
Scott, Frank 123
Scott, Stan 14
Scruggs, Mary 173
    Photos: 173
Sea Isle School 83
Sekka, Johnny 15
Senghor, Dr. Léopold Sédar 15
Seymour, Marissa 70
Seymour, Ricky 70, 197
    Photos: 70
Sheard, Bishop Drew 33
Shelby, LaRita 2, 10, 11, 39, 54, 67, 69, 224, 272, 307
    Photos: 190, 223, 275
Shelby State College 42, 43, 77
Sherman, Mrs. 39, 40
    Photos: 39
Shiloh Baptist Church 30, 50, 118

INDEX

Sigma Gamma Rho Sorority, Inc. 117
Simmons, Norbert
   Photos: 263
Simon, Reggie 224
Sims, Harold 203
Smith, Baileigh Regina
   Photos: 250
Smith, Bishop Samuel 5, 106, 107, 112
   Photos: 112, 151
Smith, Bryleigh Rose
   Photos: 250
Smith, Jada Pinkett 203
Smith, Kimberly
   Photos: 250
Smith, Lee Ella Patterson 104, 106, 111, 112
   Photos: 112, 151
Smith, Patrick
   Photos: 250
Smith, Reggie
   Photos: 246
Smith, Regina A.
   Photos: 249
Smith, Reginald Floyd, Jr. II, PhD
   Photos: 248
Smith, Reginald, III
   Photos: 250
Smith, Reginald Sr. 249
   Photos: 248
Smith, Ritta Hawkins Porter 59, 87
   Photos: 59, 64
Smith, Shirley Westbrooks 6, 135, 136, 168, 248, 249, 250
   Photos: 135, 136, 171, 240, 242, 246, 252
Smith, Stanie Robin, Sr. 87
Smith, Will 203
Soulsville Neighborhood Watch Association 117

Soul Winner's Conference Choir 108
Southside Church 107, 112
Southwest College 77
Steed, Dr. Julia Martin 50
Steen, Sammie 74, 76
Steinberg, Irv 186
Steinberg, Sidney
   Photos: 263
Step by Step @ LA 17, 207, 208
Stewart, Rod 13, 186
Stiles, Allen 93
Stiles, Dorothy Kathleen 116
Stiles, Ellen Louise Dunford
   Photos: 116
Stiles, Evelyn 117
Stiles, Mary 117
Stiles, Saint James II 117
Stiles, Sheila 117
Stone, Sly 13, 203
Student Non-Violent Coordinating Committee (SNCC) 93
Styles, Jay
   Photos: 275
Suggs Family, The 23

T

Talley, Agnes
   Photos: 234
Tatum, Rosie
   Photos: 246
Taylor, James 137, 169
Taylor, Rev. Lonzie Odie, a.k.a. L. O. 97
Temple Church of God in Christ 28, 142, 160
Temple of Deliverance 108, 111, 112, 114

Tennessee Department of Education 102

Tennessee Independent Colleges and Universities Association 40

Terry, Beatrice Bryant 41, 42

Thayard, Max
Photos: 272

Thomas, Dr. Andrew 202
Photos: 266

Thomas, Francis 160

Thomas, Moses 180

Tobin, Pat
Photos: 230

Todd, Beverly
Photos: 234

Tolbert, Lauren 50

Tombolo Maps & Design 11

Tony, Callie 173

Tony's Inn 180

Townes, Mrs. 160

Traughber, Schuyler 17

Trump, Donald 221, 222

Turner, Johnnie 94

U

United Music Heritage, Inc. 17

University of Birmingham 215

University of Indiana 218, 277, 278
Photos: 271

University of Michigan at Ann Arbor 101

Utah State University 69

V

Vanguard Award, The 17

Vincent, Dr. 97

W

Walz, Tim 222

Washburn, Professor 160
Photos: 161

Washington, Michael S. 69

Wasserman, Lew
Photos: 263

Waterford, Martha Jane Moore 81, 85

Watson, Johnny B.
Photos: 148

WBBP Radio 108

WDIA Radio 52, 200

Weaver, Alonzo 121

Weaver, Alonzo, II 126
Photos: 121

Weaver, Alonzo, III 120
Photos: 120

Weaver, Claribelle Howard 121, 122, 126, 127
Photos: 121

Weaver, Phoebe 6, 121, 126
Photos: 126

Wesson, Vivian Louise Malone 57

Westbrooks, Alice Moore 240

Westbrooks, Alicia
Photos: 242

Westbrooks, Al, Jr.
Photos: 33

Westbrooks, Alpha 11, 243

Westbrooks, Alphonso, Jr. 34, 136, 156
Photos: 156, 241, 251

Westbrooks, Alphonso, Sr. 136, 140, 163, 243
Photos: 90, 136, 201, 240

Westbrooks, Aricka 245
Photos: 244

Westbrooks, Babette 215, 216
Photos: 214, 215, 256, 261

INDEX

Westbrooks, Chaz
Photos: 243
Westbrooks Collection, Logan H. 17, 278
Westbrooks, Dr. Logan H. 1, 2, 6, 10, 12, 17, 25, 111, 170, 243, 307
Photos: 26, 148, 222, 260, 273, 277
Westbrooks, Erma Jean Bowen
Photos: 171
Westbrooks, Geri Douthet 11
Westbrooks, Gloria 136
Photos: 136, 147, 199, 240, 246
Westbrooks Helping Hands Home for Boys
Photos: 208
Westbrooks, Henry
Photos: 174
Westbrooks Management 16
Westbrooks, Pearl 6, 136, 159, 252, 254
Photos: 136, 138, 159, 161, 171, 240, 242, 246, 251
Westbrooks, Shirley 6, 135, 136, 168, 248, 249, 250
Photos: 135, 136, 171, 240, 242, 246, 248, 252
Westbrooks Village 16
Whalum, Memphian Kameron, III 29
White, Peggy
Photos: 31
Wilkes, Jamaal
Photos: 233
Wilkins, Roy 202
Williams, Dr. Daniel Hale 165
Williams, Ola Nell Moore 82
Williams, Phoebe Weaver, Esq. 6, 121, 126
Photos: 126
Willie Mitchell Studios 29
Photos: 282

Wills, Memory Kathryn Bishop 37
Wilson, Nancy 15, 202
Winters, Tony
Photos: 272
Wolof 134
Wortham, Rev. Lewis D.
Photos: 192
Wright, O. V. 29
WWRL Radio 185

X

Xzibit 209

Y

Yancy, Emily
Photos: 234
Yates, Clifford 32
Yates, Nadine 32
Yetnikoff, Walter 15
Young, Andrew 14, 203
Photos: 264
Young People Willing Workers (YPWW) 34, 107, 188
Your Hollywood Local 17
Photos: 275

The Music Business Series from Logan H. Westbrooks

  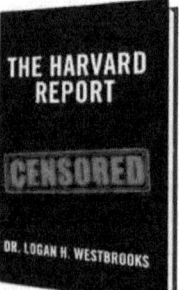

www.LoganWestbrooks.com

LAUDERDALE SUB: MEMORIES OF A MEMPHIS NEIGHBORHOOD

Designed by LaRita Shelby and White Stone Pages

Cover Concept by Dr. Logan H. Westbrooks

Additional Graphic Design by Jessica Godbee

Typeset by White Stone Pages, United Kingdom

Book printed and bound by IngramSpark, La Vergne, Tennessee

Composed in Adobe Caslon Pro

www.ingramcontent.com/pod-product-compliance
Lightning Source LLC
Chambersburg PA
CBHW071150070526
44584CB00019B/2736